Out and About

Richard Barsam

Copyright © 2025 by Richard Barsam

All rights reserved. No part of this publication may be reproduced, distributed, or transmitted in any form or by any means, including photocopying, recording, or other electronic or mechanical methods, without the prior written permission of the publisher, except in the case of brief quotations embodied in critical reviews and certain other noncommercial uses permitted by copyright law.

Table of Contents

Preface 1

Chapter One: A City In Southern California 2

Chapter Two: My Parents 18

Chapter Three: My Early Years 31

Chapter Four: Junior High School 55

Chapter Five: Sex Education 67

Chapter Six: Neighborhood Life 75

Chapter Seven: High School 90

Chapter Eight: College Life 104

Chapter Nine: Graduate School 115

Chapter Ten Coming Out 130

Chapter Eleven: Manhattan And Me: Part One 140

Chapter Twelve: Manhattan And Me: Part Two 159

Chapter Thirteen: New York's Gay Life 174

Chapter Fourteen: Edgar Munhall 184

Chapter Fifteen: People And Places 206

Chapter Sixteen: Moving On 219

Chapter Seventeen: Life With Edgar 238

Chapter Eighteen: My Life After Edgar 259

Afterword 279

Page Left Blank Intentionally

As William Trevor wrote, "Memory...forms character—the way you remember things makes you who you are."

Preface

This book chronicles the evolution of my life from my earliest years to my current life at age 86. I discuss the recurring themes that have defined my journey; consequently, it is organized chronologically with some flashforwards and flashbacks, to borrow cinematic terms. It explores growth, including the transformation of the setting from a small town in Southern California to the vastness of New York City. It tells the story of a boy who realizes early on that he may be different from others, evolving into a man who, by disclosing his homosexuality, remains distinct yet content. It highlights the role my parents played in my upbringing. It reflects on the education I received from kindergarten through university. It recounts my twelve years in college and graduate school, ultimately earning a Ph.D. It narrates my experience of coming out gay in a conservative community. It details my career as a professor and administrator at a major university, the books I have written, and the travels I have undertaken across four of the seven continents. It encompasses the people I have loved and many others who have influenced my life, especially the forty year relationship I enjoyed with one man. It shares what I have learned from my experiences and how I have applied that knowledge to pursue a good life. Thus, it is about me, an honest and comprehensive account of my life.

Chapter One:
A City In Southern California

Glendale and Its Founders

Some 90,000 years ago, archeologists say, the foundation was laid for what was to become the city of Glendale in the late 1800's. Research reveals that the Gabrielino-Tongva tribes were the first known indigenous people to inhabit the area. They, along with numerous other tribes, had established villages and ranches before 1769, the year of the first documented European exploration of the area. Its leader, Gaspar de Portolá, was subsequently appointed as the Spanish Governor of Las Californias. In 1771, Father Junípero Serra founded the first Catholic mission aimed at converting Native Americans to Catholicism.

In 1784, Spanish army officer Jose Maria Verdugo received a land grant that allowed him to establish a vast cattle ranch in this area, initially known as La Zanja, later as Rancho de los Verdugo, and, during its decline, as Rancho San Rafael. California joined the Union as the thirty-first state in 1850 as westward expansion continued. The new state government recognized that too many people claimed ownership of Rancho San Rafael, leading to a court decision known as the Great Partition of 1871, which divided the ranch into thirty-one sections allocated to twenty-eight different individuals, including some members of the Verdugo family. At the same time, the government encouraged White men to develop their own parcels of land. The significance of the Verdugo family to the region was emphasized when the mountain range behind Glendale was named the Verdugos. A historic site in Glendale is the Catalina Verdugo Adobe, an adobe house that Teodoro Verdugo, Jose Verdugo's grandson, built for his aunt Catalina.

In the late 1880s, the local population, predominantly White, adopted the name Glendale, a name with Scottish echoes. The names Glen and Dale are frequently found on maps of Scotland. The Scottish influence is further reflected in street names such as Ard Eevin, Ben Lomond, Campbell, Bruce, Cameron, Cumberland, and Lockerbie, to name just a few. Glendale—the anglicized version of the Gaelic Gleann Dail—means fertile valley, a name that attracted Midwestern farmers with its consistently good weather, diverse job opportunities, and appeal to retirees. These pragmatic individuals settled the land stretching beneath the stunning Verdugo foothills, laying it out meticulously like a prairie town, with everything aligned at right angles. By the 1920s, the prevailing aesthetic featured white shingled houses on small lots limited to one-eighth of an acre. These homes typically had ample porches at the front, accommodating a swinging divan, along with a small lawn and a concrete driveway leading to the detached one-car garage at the back of the lot, as well as space for growing flowers and keeping a few chickens or rabbits. This was long before we had what we now recognize as the typical California backyard, complete with flagstone patios, outdoor barbecue grills, and swimming pools.

Glendale's population grew from 3,500 in 1908 to 82,000 in 1940, and by 2024, it is approximately 200,000, with 72% of residents identifying as White. As this population increased, residents preserved some Midwestern architectural styles while also constructing homes that reflected the Spanish style, often referred to as Mediterranean, featuring thick stucco walls, decorative wrought iron fixtures over windows and doors, patios off main rooms, and houses oriented inward for tranquility and privacy. Today, this architectural style is common across much of Southern California, including the house we moved to when I was ten, an impressive residence on Matilija Road, just two blocks above Kenneth Road. My mother believed there were only two neighborhoods in Glendale: above Kenneth Road, which, according to the saying, was on the right side of the tracks, and below it, which was not. Living above Kenneth was seen as a mark of success. The name Matilija (pronounced mah-til-i-ha) honors the leader of the Chumash, a Native American people who settled around the same time as the previously mentioned Gabrielino-Tongva tribe.

However, no name had a greater impact on Glendale from its earliest days and throughout its continued growth than that of Leslie Coombs Brand, who was born in Missouri in 1859 and arrived in Southern California in 1886. A pioneer, he made his fortune in real estate and, after settling in Glendale, played a key role in modernizing and enhancing his new hometown. For instance, he developed the Pacific Electric Railway, which connected Glendale with nearby towns and later with downtown Los Angeles. Brand also improved telephone services, as well as gas, electrical, and water utilities. He founded the First National Bank and the Glendale Country Club. By 1887, the town was declared "the first and only rival" of its neighboring town, Pasadena. It boasted its grand Hotel Glendale, its newspaper and school system, many churches, and new housing, including several notable houses built by wealthy merchants. Glendalians took pride in the many early silent films made in the area at that time by studio units on location. However, the industry's roots were in the Edendale (now Silver Lake) area, which spilled over into Glendale, and where Charles Chaplin, Mack Sennett, Gloria Swanson, and Buster Keaton began their movie careers.

The grandest of all houses in Glendale at the time, built in 1923, was Leslie Brand's El Miradero (meaning viewpoint), an imposing mansion designed in a palace style that looks more Indian than Mexican. The locals simply referred to it as Brand's Castle. It is situated at the top of Grandview Avenue, at the corner of Mountain Road, in the Verdugo foothills, just two blocks from our house on Matilija Road, yet at first isolated above an expansive stretch of undeveloped land that reached toward the distant Hollywood Hills. Surrounded by high white walls and a massive, guarded gateway, this castle featured orchards, an airplane landing strip capable of servicing five planes, a swimming pool, and a tennis court. Brand, who passed away in 1925, was laid to rest in a pyramid-shaped tomb in the family cemetery on the property, while his dogs had their own burial ground. The Brands did not have children, so after his death, the entire estate was opened to the public. In the 1950s, my friends and I spent countless hours playing there, hiking into the ranch's backcountry (home to rattlesnakes), staging mock ceremonies around his tomb, and peeking through the windows of the main house, which had been stripped of all furnishings. Following his wife's death in 1945, the land and castle, according to his will, became the property of the City of Glendale, with the house transforming into the arts branch of the Glendale Public Library, where many years later, my mother, an excellent cook, was invited to offer classes in Armenian cuisine.

Racial History

Race relations are a significant and challenging issue in Glendale's history. In 2020, the City Council passed a resolution apologizing for its racist past as a Sundown Town, where Black, Brown, and Asian workers living elsewhere were expected to leave the city by sundown or risk police action or imprisonment. To further their humiliation, they were also barred from residing in or purchasing property anywhere in the city. This was the reality when I was growing up, indeed throughout most of the 20th century. I only had to step outside our house around five o'clock P.M. to see the housekeepers, handymen, and gardeners rushing down the hill to catch a bus before sundown if they weren't driving out of the city in their own cars. There were also incidents of anti-Semitism, although Jews could buy property, live in Glendale, and attend their synagogue. Nevertheless, there was an unspoken discrimination against Jews, as you will read later.

Outside forces also shaped Glendale's racial history. As we have seen, the Spanish and Indigenous people who founded it were marginalized and eventually replaced by White settlers. Leslie Brand was a staunch conservative who not only played a key role in Glendale's economic development but also in its racial history. Generally, Americans associate the Ku Klux Klan with the Southern states, but Brand, who was born in Missouri, strongly supported the organization, even offering the grounds of his castle to the local KKK branch for their gatherings. This walled property did not ensure total secrecy, according to my father. He recalled that in the mid-'20s, he went with his brother and friends to observe one of these events. Concealing themselves among the trees and bushes that bordered the airfield, they saw men on horseback in white gowns and hoods, carrying burning torches and riding past crosses that were staked into the ground. In 1924, according to a report in the Los Angeles Times, 350 new members were "naturalized" into the order, a ceremony held on the airport runway and witnessed one evening by about 3,000 order members.

Glendale's racial history arose from animosity towards anyone who was not White. In the 1920s, as millions of European and Asian immigrants came to the United States, most chose to settle in major cities where more job opportunities existed compared to smaller towns like Glendale. However, ethnic immigrants often gravitate toward areas where their communities are already established, and several affluent Armenian families moved to Glendale, including the Ignatius and Jamgochian families, with whom the Barsam family had close ties. They were not the first Armenians in the area and certainly would not be the last. These two families had the means to maintain a comfortable lifestyle, reside in grand homes in the best neighborhoods, and send their children to prestigious private colleges. Paul Ignatius, whose father was my father's great-uncle, attended the University of Southern California and then Harvard. He served as Secretary of the Navy under the Kennedy administration and concluded his career as the President of the Washington Post newspaper.

As early as the 1920s, Glendale had been designated an "All-American" city, and a closer look at its citizens reveals the same racial prejudice that was evident across the nation. It took another three decades before the city acted. Even then, Glendale was slow to comply with the civil rights legislation enacted during and after the Truman administration. While there was a minor effort to ban discrimination in public housing and transportation, as late as 1960, Glendale remained a sundown town, except that it allowed these non-White workers to live at their workplaces.

In 1964, George Lincoln Rockwell, the founder of the American Nazi Party (ANP), relocated his headquarters to Glendale. When asked why he chose Glendale, he responded, "I understand Glendale is a White man's town. The most American. The best in terms of Americanism." The group remained for two years until the city leadership, embarrassed by the negative attention highlighting the town's reputation for racial discrimination, officially evicted them. I recall that their run-down building was near Bob's Big Boy, a drive-in restaurant that was a favorite for teenagers on Friday nights. We would drive by and yell insults at the place as we made our way to Bob's for burgers. In time, both the KKK and the ANP were expelled from Glendale, yet it continued to be a racist community.

In the 1970s, after I moved to New York, I mentioned to an African-American colleague that I was from Glendale. He told me that he had heard The Rev. Martin Luther King, Jr. refer to it as Lily-White Glendale. My research into King's papers and speeches did not yield any evidence of such a remark, but it may have been a casual comment that stuck in the public's mind. Regardless, it was a relevant description, and discrimination persists today, as seen in Glendale's school cafeterias, where it has been reported that white students eat at one table, non-white students at another, and Armenians at yet another. As recently as 2020, Glendale woke up to become the first city in California, and the third in the nation, to pass a resolution apologizing for racial exclusion. The newly formed Coalition for an Anti-Racist Glendale promised "to address institutional and structural racism by identifying harmful patterns and practices that directly impact the lives of Black, Indigenous, and People of Color in Glendale."

In 2024, as I write, 40% of Glendale's population is Armenian. Since Armenians are White and Christian, they have faced little opposition to their businesses, schools, and churches in the city, and they are accepted to the point that overt prejudice is not currently an issue. However, my sister, who lives in Glendale, tells me that many current residents resent the influx of immigrants identifying as

Armenians who come from Russia, Lebanon, and Iran. They are tarnishing the reputation of full-blooded Armenians.

If there was any racism in my immediate family, I can speak only of the years when I was growing up and at home, close to my mother most of the day, and did not know about racial prejudice or racist words. She spent her first thirteen years with a French-speaking family in Canada and then moved to an English-speaking family in Pasadena, California. Whether there was racism in that family, I have no idea, but Pasadena was larger and more racist than its neighbor Glendale, so we can imagine that she may have heard from her Pasadena family ideas and words she did not know or fully understand. Perhaps she did understand them and believe in them, I don't know, but she did pass some of it down to me. As a youth, I heard her use the "N" word. For example, she was an enthusiastic gardener and often spent several hours caring for her plants, and when she had finished, and came into the house and said, "I'm exhausted; I've been working all day like a nigger." She meant working like a slave and usually said it jokingly, as the word was then in familiar use. When she caught me putting a coin into my mouth, she reprimanded me with, "Take that out. A nigger may have touched it." As the years passed, she stopped using that word or making any other racist comments. I do not recall her using any racist words against Hispanics or Asians, and my father never used a racist word in front of me. However, as you will read later on, my mother's deeply ingrained prejudice against Blacks hurt me deeply.

My first personal experience with prejudice happened when I was 12. Near our house, there was a large property owned by the Swedenborg family, which included a main house for Mrs. Swedenborg, the matriarch, and a ranch house for her son's family. The estate was surrounded by a tall iron fence, with access secured by an electric gate. I didn't know anyone in the family except for William, a boy our age who sometimes played with us. To our surprise, we all received formal invitations to a pool party for his birthday. Refreshments and gift opening were to follow the swimming. None of us had ever been inside this property, although we often trespassed harmlessly into others, so we agreed to go as a group.

At the party, I was having a great time splashing around when Grandmother Swedenborg ordered me to get out of the water because, in her words, she "didn't allow New Yorkers in her pool." I had been behaving myself in the pool, not doing anything wrong, and I couldn't imagine why I was being singled out to leave. I told her that I was born in Glendale and had never been to New York, but that John Stoppard (not his real name), a close neighbor boy, was born there, and maybe she had confused me with him. His father was known to be Jewish, but not his mother, so John could not be considered Jewish. No, she said, I was to leave immediately. John stayed at the party.

I went home, bewildered and humiliated, after being thrown out of a party to which I was invited. When I told my father what had happened, he needed to call a friend to understand that the term "New Yorkers" referred to Jews. He wasted no time in walking to the

Swedenborgs' gate and asking to see Mrs. Swedenborg. They spoke, and he made it clear that the Barsams were neither New Yorkers nor Jews, for whom he had the highest regard, adding that her treatment of me was an insult to the entire community. He took no further action, but there was no apology from the Swedenborg family. My friends and I avoided associating with William, who was soon sent to a boarding school.

Assimilation and Conformity

For my parents, assimilation into a new country and culture was an important goal, but they shouldn't have chosen an unsuitable place like Glendale. Living there was a challenge for them, as it is a Los Angeles suburb where the residents were almost entirely White, Christian, and ultra-conservative in their political views. While there was a small Jewish population, there were no Asian, Black, or Brown people. The residents knew little, if anything, about Armenians and their history, which includes Armenia becoming the first nation to adopt Christianity as a state religion and the Armenians' suffering centuries of persecution for their beliefs while trying to co-exist in the surrounding Muslim world. I encountered such cultural ignorance one day when a neighbor, Mr. O'Neil, asked where my parents were from. Upon learning that we were Armenians, he replied, "Ah, you're the folks who eat the lamb." "The lamb" is a curious usage that has a chilling effect, similar to saying that the Jews "are the people who killed Jesus."

Glendale was a place of widespread conformity; indeed, it was a temple of conformity. In the 1950s, with the popularity of Sloan Wilson's novel The Man in the Grey Flannel Suit and the film adapted from it, the story represents the post-war generation grappling with contemporary cultural values. It depicts a corporate world that takes precedence over individuality, where men dress alike in grey flannel suits and engage in a rat race to achieve and maintain a perfect job and income, a perfect home, perfect children, and a perfect wife in a perfect little community of similar people, all defined by their adherence to those norms.

I was a high school student back then, surrounded by conformity in nearly every aspect of school life. I understand small-town conformity and recognize that it has its place in the lives of millions. I am not a conformist and prefer individuality, flexibility, originality, and competition—just a few of the factors that make living in Manhattan so exciting for me.

My father and mother understood the importance, power, and necessity of conformity and managed to sustain a lifestyle that was appropriate for our neighborhood. There is no doubt that they faced social rejection from a few snobbish neighbors, but that did not bother them. Dad contributed to the community by working as an Air Raid Warden during World War II (he was too old to be drafted or enlist), and together with my mother, they participated in school and community organizations. He admired the work of the Masonic Order but never joined and was a member of the Kiwanis Club for several years. He played golf with neighbors but was not the country club type. He also attended Mormon church services and briefly considered becoming a member because he was impressed with their charitable efforts. Both my mother and father were friendly, sociable people known for their exceptional hospitality. Any conformity they might have sought did not come at the expense of their values.

Eventually, Glendale went through a significant transformation, not only in its population growth but also in its diversity. In 2024, Glendale's total population was about 200,000. Of this number, approximately 71% are White (of which 35% identify as Armenians), 18% are Hispanic or Latino, 13% are Asian, 2% are Black or African American, 0.4% are American Indian and Alaska Native, and 0.1% are Native Hawaiian and Other Pacific Islander.

The Glendale Way of Life in the 1940s and 1950s

When I was growing up in the 1940s and 50s, Glendale was still small and safe enough for a young boy to roam freely. I traveled on foot, by car, or by bus to places like Fremont Park, Nibley Park, and the Verdugo Pool. California law allowed a 12-year-old to obtain a learner's driving permit, and after passing the test, I was driving our station wagon around town by the age of 13. My parents asked me to limit my driving to our immediate neighborhood, so I took the bus to the Verdugo Pool, a large outdoor pool far across town, where I honed the swimming skills I had learned at the YMCA. When she had time, my mother would drive me to my piano lessons in a downtown building in Glendale. The teacher was Mr. Field, a man devoted to American music but also a creep for making inappropriate advances toward me. After a year of being pawed and pursued in his studio, I quit and lied to my parents, saying that I had learned everything I could from him.

The houses in Glendale ranged from tidy bungalows to elegant mansions; its schools were among the best in California, and its population consisted mainly of second-generation Protestants born in Glendale—WASPs, in the literal sense of that acronym. That profile of the city has changed, of course, but the majority remains well-off in economic terms. There has always been a significant amount of money in the town earned by executives in the movie and aeronautics industries in nearby Burbank and Hollywood. Today, the average annual household income in Glendale is $107,000, while the median household income is $80,000 per year. The high earners reside in impressive homes built in new subdivisions in the once-unspoiled Verdugo Hills. For that social set in the 1950s, Glendale boasted the Oakmont Country Club, the oldest and still most exclusive organization, where membership is, and has always been, by invitation only. Today, two other country clubs focus on sports and social events, each featuring an eighteen-hole golf course. In a recent review of their websites, the photographs depicted only White members.

Today's Glendale features a vibrant commercial area; however, when I was younger, shopping was confined to just a few blocks along Brand Boulevard. There was one large department store, Webb's, along with many smaller shops. For more extensive shopping options, one had to travel to Pasadena or downtown Los Angeles. Now, I understand that the Glendale Galleria is the third-largest shopping mall in Los Angeles County.

As I grew up, I remember Glendale as a God-fearing community, where Sunday church attendance felt almost mandatory for both parents and children. My parents were not religious, but they believed my sister and I should become familiar with a church and make our own decisions. I was enrolled in Sunday school at the North Glendale Methodist Church, where I joined a group of children gathering in a room for Sunday school while their parents attended services. I joined the choir and participated in those services. Shortly afterward, in elementary school, my parents discouraged me from attending a religious meeting on Thursday afternoons, which was an unofficial part of the curriculum. Later, during high school, I attended the Grandview Presbyterian Church, a fundamentalist Christian church, but I quickly lost interest. My genuine curiosity about religion emerged in college, where I attended Episcopalian services offered to students. Even then, I wasn't sure if religion would or should play a role in my life. Today, Glendale's religious affiliations have diversified, with 53% of residents identifying with a religion: 50% are Christians, 1.1% are Jews, and 2% are Muslims, Buddhists, or Hindus.

Regarding politics, Glendale, during my time, was known as a staunchly Republican city. Indeed, in 1961, when I first voted, my parents and I went to the polling place, and the officials there, all neighbors, jokingly called out, "Here they come," meaning, they said, that we were the only Democrats voting in that precinct. Such a scenario could not happen now, as during the 2020 presidential election, 70% of the voters identified as Democrats, while 30% were Republicans. It may have taken around sixty years to reach this point, but it is now a more diverse and tolerant town than ever before.

Chapter Two:
My Parents

This chapter introduces my parents, Suren and Marie Barsam. Knowing their background should help you to better understand them.

The Armenian people have existed since pre-historic times in the region surrounding the Biblical Mountain of Ararat. The Kingdom of Armenia was founded in 600 BCE, and in 301 CE, it became the first country in the world to adopt Christianity as its official state religion. Subsequently, its twin desires for autonomy and religious freedom, unfortunately, provoked their rivals to conquest and domination. In 1045, Armenia was conquered by the Byzantine empire; in 1230, by the Mongols; and, in the 1500s, by the Ottoman empire. These Ottoman rulers granted the Armenians considerable autonomy, making it possible for them to live as distinct enclaves, nevertheless within Turkey's boundaries, and not in their own country. They continued to suffer the discrimination they had endured through the centuries, to be exploited in the worst possible way as the Ottoman Empire began to collapse in the first decade of the 20th century. In 1915, shortly after the start of WWI, the Turkish government unleashed an organized program of ruthless torture and killing directed at these residents, a systematized massacre that resulted in the deaths of 1.5 million Armenians. Identified as the first modern genocide, it is said to have influenced Hitler's solution to his "Jewish Question" a few years later.

My Mother's Story

My parents were born in the city of Harpoot (often spelled Harput), an Armenian enclave in Turkey. Their stories begin in the years before the First World War (1914-1918). My mother, Marie Louise, was born in 1914, the daughter of Hovnan and Nazalie Sarafian Pashgian, the youngest of six children, including two other daughters—Armenouhi, who eventually moved to New York City, and Berjouhi, who remained in Beirut along with their brothers, Sarkis and Samuel. Nothing is known of Arsen, a third brother. My mother was too young in 1918 to remember much of the massacre in which her mother was killed. And, according to relatives who knew the story, her father deserted the family after the massacres (perhaps even before) and re-appeared years later in Los Angeles. It's likely that his brother John in Pasadena, knowing that Hovnan had abandoned his family, refused to accept him back into the Pashgian family. Almost nothing is known of Hovnan's years in California, but his death was reported in this October 5, 1919, article in the Los Angeles Times, titled "Grief Leads to Suicide":

Brooding over the massacre by the Turks of his wife and two sons in Armenia and the rumors of further Turkish outrages against Armenians are believed by the relatives here of H [Hovnan]. S. Pashgian, whose body was found in the ocean at Santa Monica yesterday, to have unbalanced his mind. . . . H. S. Pashgian had been in America about eight years. His family was massacred before he came to this country. He had lived alone in the northern part of the city for a number of years.

Doing the numbers, we can guess that he deserted his family as early as 1911 and entered the United States in that same year. My father occasionally heard rumors about his brother-in-law being seen in Armenian social circles in Los Angeles, but nothing more is known. If my mother knew any of this history, she never mentioned it, and my father protected her by forbidding me and my sister to ask her any questions that might upset her. Likewise, her Pasadena family also kept silent on the subject.

Sometime during the war, Marie was sent to the Birds' Nest Orphanage in the Lebanese city of Byblos, operated by a Danish organization founded specifically for the relocation of Armenian orphans to Lebanon and other countries. Thanks to the Armenian Immigration Project, we know that on July 7, 1927, when Marie was 13, she sailed on the "Sinaia" from Beirut—via Jaffa, Palestine, and Piraeus, Greece—to Providence, Rhode Island, and thence by train to the Armenian Boys' Farm in Georgetown, Ontario, Canada, an institution, that despite its name, sheltered both orphaned boy and girl survivors of the genocide and helped them to secure homes in Canada. She was placed with the Weir family in Vancouver, B.C., where she lived for several happy years. Mrs. Weir became her surrogate mother, not only teaching her to speak fluent French but also to cook French cuisine. Eventually, she reached the age of 13, which qualified her for entry into the U.S., which was sponsored by her uncle John Pashgian of Pasadena, whose sister Haiganoush was my father's mother. Thus, the ties between the Barsamian and Pashgian families were intertwined, at least on paper.

Uncle John was a rug merchant, renowned, especially among wealthy people in the movie business, for offering the finest Middle Eastern carpets on the West Coast. Moreover, for his charitable work in Pasadena, he and his wife, Rosa Constantian, became models of upper-class respectability. He and his brother Moses were part of the group of businesspeople who founded the Pasadena Rose Parade, still held annually on New Year's Day. The Pashgian family lived in an impressive mansion overlooking the city, and the three Pashgian children enjoyed all the material, cultural, and educational opportunities of their status. Yet they did not regard my mother as their equal or offer her the same opportunities. They may have been making her pay for the shame that her father's behavior caused them. Indeed, she was a Cinderella figure, given a small bedroom off the kitchen and expected, in a house with a cook and servants, to help with household tasks. She never complained about this, but it certainly would affect any teenage girl. As for her formal education, she was surpassed by her two step-brothers, who went to Stanford University, and the step-sister, who attended Bryn Mawr College. Mother, however, had theatrical ambitions, so she attended Pasadena City College to study theater and later continued her study at the Pasadena Play House, a famous laboratory of theatrical experimentation and production, which had trained many theater and film actors. But my mother then wanted more from life than life was willing to give her, and her theatrical aspirations were not fulfilled.

My Father's Story

My father's much different background is recounted here as well as in My Story: Coming to America, privately published for family and friends. It is a detailed account of the ordeal he endured from the time of his birth to the day he entered the USA. Both of his parents were born into prosperous families that had been annihilated. My paternal grandfather, Avedis Barsam (the original name Barsamian was shortened for business reasons), was a prosperous merchant in international trade as well as an influential politician. His wife, Haiganoush Ignatiosian [Ignatius], was a member of the Ignatius family, some of whom eventually moved to Glendale. Father's siblings were Meran, Khoren, Karekin, Zaven, and sister Takoohi. Suren and Meran were the only ones to survive the massacre. Sometime before 1915, Meran emigrated to the United States and later was instrumental in bringing his little brother to the USA. The only official record of Suren's birth, his 1928 Certificate of Naturalization, lists his age as 25, implying that he was born on July 15, 1903. Although he did not really know either the date or year of his birth, he consistently said that it was mid-July in 1903. However, by his saying he was nine years old at the time of the massacre, it is more likely that he was born three years later.

At the age of nine, he miraculously survived the massacre, even as he watched the male members of the family slaughtered, and several days later, when he thought it might be safe, he saw his mother and sister jump into a deep well to their deaths. Although he became an orphan in 1915, he did not then have the advantage, like my mother, of being saved by an orphanage. He was essentially on his own and suffered a challenging ordeal to survive amongst the murderous Turks who thought nothing about the fate of the Armenians remaining in Turkey. Between the ages of 9 and 15, he walked more than 3,000 miles across Turkey, working on farms to get food and using his skill with horses to improve his worth to those who took him in. Notable among them was a German female doctor who took him in, housed and fed him, put him in charge of her horses, and later helped him to reach Constantinople (now Istanbul). But getting there proved to be another dangerous ordeal, for what was ordinarily a four-day journey took him three months. During his entire life, his only formal education was at Robert College in Constantinople, founded by American Christian missionaries. Here he began to plan his trip to the U.S.A. and learned to speak Arabic, Armenian, Turkish, as well as some English, and while he earned and saved money from working at all kinds of jobs, he was repeatedly robbed of most of it. The college staff helped him to contact his brother Meran in America. In 1921, when he was 15, Meran sent him money for travel, but it too was stolen. Two more years would pass before October 1923 when Papa, at age 17, boarded the "Roussillon," a ship from Marseilles bound for New York City. As it did for most emigrants, his ticket gave him a spot on the floor in steerage, where he said conditions were so awful that he spent much of his time on deck. To keep up his spirits, he told me of watching the porpoises that followed the ship, reading the Bible from beginning to end, and surviving on a diet of bread and water.

Finally setting foot on Ellis Island in October 1923, he remembers the health exams and endurance tests that were given to screen immigrants who might be sick. On a more cheerful note, he was given a banana, something he'd never seen, and didn't know what to do with until he was encouraged to eat it. Thus, standing on American soil, wearing a suit he bought for just this moment, he was ready for his new life. Because he continually repeated the word "Boston," the authorities sent him to Grand Central Terminal, where he was put on a train for that destination. But, meanwhile, his brother had taken a train from Boston to New York. Thus, confusion reigned for a few days until they finally had their reunion, an emotional climax to years of fear and uncertainty. The two brothers then traveled by train first to Boston and then to Meran's home in Cincinnati.

In Ohio, Meran established a successful clothing manufacturing company, and Suren joined him. However, the business did not prosper, and they moved to Los Angeles. In 1928, my father became a naturalized U.S. citizen. The two brothers started another venture, manufacturing sportswear for women, but that business floundered and died in the desperate economy of the Great Depression.

Meran and his wife Hazel had two children, Betty and Meran Avedis, known as Bud. attended Glendale High School, the rival school to mine, where he was a football player and a popular campus figure. As for Betty, after working at the clothing factory, she married motion picture producer William M. Graf, with whom she enjoyed a fascinating life. But tragedy struck that wing of the Barsam family when, in the early thirties, father Meran was instantly killed by a hit-

and-run driver on a Glendale street. Then, during WW II, on August 27, 1943, Bud Barsam, 2nd Lieutenant and co-pilot of the B-17 bomber "Shangrila Lil," was shot down near the Belgian border. Of the crew of ten, three were killed, including Bud; the other seven were captured as POW's. His body was never found. I was four when we got the news and I remember the effect it had on our family, especially the day when a uniformed soldier appeared at our house to present us with the huge American flag that symbolized his military service. I took the flag, sat on the floor, and wept. During the depression, Papa had established a laundry and dry-cleaning business through a very profitable contract with Paramount Pictures for providing the clothes cleaning services required by studio of its size. He was at the studio checking on business matters there, when he was introduced to director Rouben Mamoulian, a fellow Armenian, whose secretary, Armenouhi Pashgian, was mother's sister. Small world. She may have persuaded Mamoulian to assign Marie a part in his current production just to keep her happy, the musical western movie High, Wide, and Handsome (1937) starring Randolph Scott and Irene Dunne. Mother was on the screen for exactly twenty-three seconds, not much of a debut. Finally, Papa discouraged her from pursuing this career by saying it was either the movies or him, but not both. Papa knew what a complicated and cruel world Hollywood was, and he protected her from disappointment. But it's an amusing irony that he was the one who got a contract from the studio, not for acting but for his livelihood.

On September 27, 1934, Suren and Marie married in a grand wedding held at the Pashgian home, and after a honeymoon at Laguna Beach, they settled in Glendale. Suren had proved himself a reliable and acceptable son-in-law to John Pashgian, for both believed in the American dream, ambition, hard work, and loyalty to his family, friends, and country. After establishing himself in America, my father's life centered on his family. He was a faithful husband, a strong father, and a generous provider of life's necessities (which, alas, did not include the electric train set I craved as a boy). Papa knew the value of money and lived within his income, scorning credit and paying cash for everything, including cars and houses. Before WWII, he bought a large parcel of land in the barren San Fernando Valley and later sold it at an astonishing profit. He then invested in major motion pictures in association with William Graf, his niece's husband, and this investment also proved rewarding. He did not mention this investment to anyone in the family, except to me, for he didn't want to associate himself with the notorious movie colony. However, he was generous in lending money to those who needed it, especially new immigrants, no matter their origin. All in all, coming out of hardship, he created a good life for his family, and although he did not fulfill his dream to be an architect, his other achievements made us all very proud.

Assimilating in a New World

The citizens of Glendale were not only ultra-conservative in their political views but also generally suspicious of all immigrants. Nevertheless, Papa did his part in the community, such as working as an Air Raid Warden during the Second World War. He was too old to be drafted or to enlist. When it came to taking part in school and community organizations, he was not a joiner and let my mother do that work. The two of them were friendly, sociable people who liked to dance at the monthly parties given by the Armenian Allied Arts Association and to entertain frequently at home.

Throughout his life, this kind, gentle man met new challenges with the same courage and strength that helped him survive his early years. He was devastated when my mother died in 1982 at the age of 68. Because he had suffered a partial loss of vision, he became dependent on his wife, a role that was assumed by his daughter, Sue. As a self-reliant and self-made man, one who believed he could always take care of himself, this dependency on others was his greatest fear in life. In these final years, my sister was not only a great comfort to him by encouraging to take life day by day and to be enthusiastic about what each day held. He put his traumatic early years in perspective, was justifiably proud of his many accomplishments, and left a rich legacy of courage for his children. My affection was stronger for my father than for anyone else.

My mother, by contrast, was a more complicated person. She was an artist whose high ambitions were finally realized when she became an expert at the arts of enameling on copper and those of Ikebana, Japanese flower arranging. She won numerous honors in both pursuits. Her beautiful hands, weakened in later years by crippling arthritis, could do anything from grafting one camelia plant onto another or making the best dinner you ever ate. She worked hard to gain approval and acceptance from the ladies in her social environment, who were set in their ways, and long devoted to good causes. She may have been overly concerned with her image in other people's opinions. She did not have a real mother to guide her, although Mrs. Weir in Vancouver was a surrogate mother, and her stepmother in Pasadena, Rosa Pashgian, whom we called Grandma Rosa, had earlier a significant influence on her. But I believe that she remained conscious that her Pasadena family, despite their bloodline, did not regard her as their equal. In her final years, her rewards came with the acceptance of her artwork, caring for her husband, and the pleasure of being the grandmother of Jennifer. Although she once had a minor heart attack when falling down stairs, she was basically healthy all her life, so her death from pancreatic cancer in 1982, age 67, was a great shock to all who knew and loved her. Father died a few years later.

My Mother and Me

No matter what our situation—time or place—nothing will let me escape examining the problematic relationship between my mother and me. Since she played an important and not always positive influence on me, I tried to understand her then and continue to be bothered now. I know that she was herself influenced by Aunt Ida Barsam, an otherwise wonderful person but one who had almost no opportunity to observe the real me. Born in Iowa, raised on a farm, and marrying an Armenian businessman at an early did not make her a worldly person. Yet when I would deliberately overhear their conversations, I heard Ida steering my mother into thinking falsehoods about me. Although my mother had other reasonable expectations for me, she did not consider me as an All-American Boy. She called me "sissy" and demanded that I "be a man, like your father." That was in the 1950s, yet today, we are still debating what "masculinity" means as a frame of reference for discussing identity. Is there such a thing as a "real man"? What ideal was I failing to meet? She worried that I would not marry, have children, and carry forward the Barsam name. She frequently predicted that I would have a lonely life. Moreover, she was concerned about what "the neighbors will think," no matter what the issue. Perhaps this was why I was not ready at any time, from my teenage years to the year when I left home for good, to tell her that I believed I was a homosexual. The closest I got to that was saying that I wanted to see a psychiatrist to better help me understand myself. Her response (worthy of comedian Gracie Allen) was, "It's all in your head." In my high school years, I was dating girls, several of whom I brought home for her to meet, but I also brought home some male friends. Much later in years, she was motherly with the three men that I loved —Mark, Jon, and Edgar— and from the closeness of these relationships, she surely knew I was gay but suppressed it out of concern for what people would think. It's my fault that she never openly accepted me as a gay man. I will discuss this more fully in Chapter 10.

In my view, my parents—who stood apart confidently from some of my friends' parents—were ideal, always there to give attention, care, and advice, but also, the older I got, to let me make my own choices and mistakes. Together, they were a model for a perfect marriage, in close communication on all matters, scornful of divorce and those couples who use it without trying to save their marriage, and themselves loyal, loving, and happy until the end. In love, they were ardent; in politics, democrats; in travel, eager to see the world; in hospitality, the most gracious and generous; in drinking, bourbon; in smoking, he always, she never; in dancing, astonishing; in gardening, active and attentive; in driving, not so good; in arguing, never, unless in private where I couldn't hear them.

Chapter Three:
My Early Years

I wish you could have shared my childhood with me, for I was a very happy boy. In one backward-looking view, my life has been a life of pictures, from the photos produced by the boxy, black Kodak that my parents used to record my early years to the sleek motion picture cameras that made the movies that occupy so much of my writing later. Pictures are memories. I'll give you a written and visual account of those years, from my birth to the end of elementary school.

I was born in the Glendale Research Hospital on November 8, 1938, at 4:10 P.M. My parents had waited for my birth through three miscarriages, and one can only imagine their relief when they had a healthy, 5 lb., 10-3/4 oz. baby boy. In fact, my father was so overcome that he fainted when told the news. The name on my birth certificate, Richard Meran Barsam, reflects my mother's choice of Richard (after Richard I, the Lion-Hearted King of England) and my father's choice of Meran (after his brother's first name).

Four years later, my sister Susan Marsha Barsam was born on July 3, 1941. Sue was a tiny, healthy infant, weighing some 4 lbs. and 8 oz., so small that my parents joked that they carried her home in a shoe box. I was then 3 years old and, unlike some children who are jealous about having a new sibling in the family, I was delighted in having her in the house and being able, in my small way, to help look after her. In February 1965, Sue and Tom Van Dalsen were married and remained living in Glendale. Their daughter, Jennifer, was born in 1973. Tom died in 2018, and Sue has adjusted in the true Barsam style, determined to continue to live a good life. She has faithful friends, some of whom date back to elementary school, and enjoys entertaining them. She phones me every Sunday morning, and we discuss the films we've seen in the past week—she is an avid movie fan—and the books we've read, friends we've had dinner with, as well as contemporary politics and the state of the world.

A few more words about Jennifer. After graduating from college, she moved to San Francisco to take a job in a publishing firm. She was well trained there in book production, and after a few years, she moved to Manhattan and worked in book production at The Metropolitan Museum of Art, where she helped to produce beautiful exhibition catalogs. She married Tor Braham, a lawyer, and they moved to Saratoga, California, where she also became the stepmother of two children, both of whom were soon graduated from college. Jennifer is active in leading a group of volunteers to maintain a bookstore for used books, where the proceeds go to help fund the local public library. She and I stay close in touch through phone calls she makes to me every Sunday afternoon. Our conversations are lively, and she remains very interested in my life in Manhattan.

The Barsam family was small, and since I do not have children to pass on the name, Sue and I are the last of the Barsams. The Barsam legacy, as my parents have left us with it, was both material and moral. We were raised to be thoughtful, helpful, good children and to be proud of who we are and the legacy from which we came. I hope I have held up my end of the bargain and made my parents proud, wherever they may be. My sister will leave a record of doing good deeds for family, neighbors, and friends. She may not have written any books, but she has made beautiful, hand-crafted quilts. She has a short fuse and can be ornery, but nevertheless, she is honest and trustworthy. And, perhaps most important of all, she was a wonderful wife and continues to be a wonderful mother and sister.

The Neighborhoods in Which I Matured

The following account begins in 1942 when I was four years old. We lived on North Pacific Avenue in Glendale, a neighborhood that was both residential and small businesses. In New York, many merchants had a store at street level and lived above it in an apartment, "living above the store" as was commonly said. In Glendale, we lived beside my father's dry-cleaning store but on the same ground level. The one-story stucco house consisted of a living room facing the lawn, two bedrooms, a kitchen and laundry room, and what was known as a sunroom, which doubled as a dining room. But my father understood what it meant to live above or even behind the shop and wanted a free-standing house in a prime residential neighborhood. That wish was fulfilled when we moved later to Matilija Road.

If you were coming to visit us in that first house, you would enter either through the front door or you could drive via an unpaved alley at the back of the property into our driveway. If you did not turn and continued to the end of the alley, you would end at a row of garages on the far side of an empty lot that bordered our property. Our fenced-in backyard was a wonderful place to play, as was the empty lot, which may have been an eyesore to adults, but kids loved it. We spotted all kinds of birds and insects there and found among the weeds such discarded things as broken bicycles and discarded appliances. I was fascinated with empty food cans and other household cast-offs, as well as abandoned houses and derelict empty lots. My most indelible memory of that lot came from the moment when, early on a Christmas morning, I looked out and saw my mother walking across the lot with my first bicycle, carrying it from its hiding place into our house. Several years later, after we moved to our new house, this property was transformed into a large building containing a U. S. Post Office, ground floor space for business establishments, including the dry-cleaning store. It was the first commercial property my father owned.

There were few children of my age in that immediate neighborhood, and I was too young to wander away in search of playmates. My parents had a strict code of behavior for me that prohibited such behavior. On a typical day, I would spend time with my mother, listening to her read to me and then later reading by myself. This helped to develop my lifetime devotion to all kinds of books. At the time, though, I enjoyed adventure stories and Jean and Laurent de Brunhoff's wonderful books about the adventures of Babar, the baby elephant, and his delightful friend, "the Old Lady." These classics of visual and literary interest are as fresh today as they were then. There was a swing set was in the backyard as well as an adult-size playhouse, which we used as a chicken pen during the war.

Although I was permitted to visit the houses of those children whose parents were familiar with mine, I was not permitted otherwise to wander around the neighborhood until I got my first bicycle at the age of nine. By then, of course, my "baby sister" (as I called her) was four years old and discovering for herself the delights in the backyard, where she played with her dolls. Our nearby playmates included the two daughters of the Baird family, who lived in a separate house that was wedged in behind a two-story apartment house, where the Icenogle family, who came from hillbilly country in the South, including two children, a girl called Billie Mae, and her younger brother, Stevie. He liked to brag that it was his chore to pluck the feathers off the chickens they bought at the farm market. Shee-kuns, as he pronounced the name, prompted an impersonation that my father would perform whenever we reminisced about that neighborhood.

While I can picture the sights of this Pacific Avenue neighborhood, I can also call up its sounds. There were the usual automobile horns and the distinctive bell every three days of the Helm's Bakery truck, luring customers with its offering of loaves of bread and other baked goods, an innovative bakery on wheels. The driver was dressed in a uniform with a patch that reminded you that Helm's was one of the sponsors of the 1932 Los Angeles Olympics. His routine was to stop the panel truck, open the back doors, and pull out trays of baked goodies for the customers to see. He sometimes offered us a free cookie. After ringing up the sales, he would drive to the next block and repeat this, with the distinctive bell announcing his arrival. These sights and sounds are vivid in my memory, as were the clear, blue skies, which we enjoyed long before the 1950s when Los Angeles County began to suffer from smog and its dirty brown fumes. The few stores within reach included a five-and-dime store, a hardware store, a pharmacy that had a soda fountain where one sat on stools and enjoyed the malts and sodas, two gas stations, and at the end of this commercial block, the Barbara Worth Market, owned by the D'Ambras family. Just around the corner from the market was the Rifken Fur Salon, owned by the only Jewish residents we knew. I spent a lot of time with Mike Rifken, a brilliant mathematics student in high school. At the opposite end of Pacific Avenue, closest to our house, one could board the Pacific Electric Red Car and arrive in downtown Los Angeles in about thirty minutes. We would take that ride when he took me to have dinner with him at Mike Lyman's Grill, an upscale restaurant that he favored. He used to joke about the restaurant's radio ad that emphasized that their potato cakes were made with "real potatoes, not substitutes." My father, amused by this, asked, "What is the substitute for a potato?"

My mother devoted these years to our house and raising her children. Her code of behavior was reinforced by punishment ranging from the denial of sweets for minor infractions to major violations like straying away from the house or using bad language. When I first used the word shit in front of her, the punishment was awful: she wiped the inside of my mouth with cayenne pepper. It only happened once, but when my father learned that I had stolen a candy bar from the dime store, he gave me a beating with his leather belt that I never forgot. The pain lasted, but I understood that my foolish misdeed was not only a petty crime but, more importantly, could tarnish our family's reputation in the neighborhood. In any event, these punishments strengthened my understanding of my parents. They were two wonderful people, deeply concerned with assimilating the family into the neighborhood and not causing trouble for anyone. When our parents went out for the evening, they hired Mrs. Tronowski, a massive Polish woman who lived nearby, to sit with my sister and me. She had all the charm of an Army sergeant and spanked us, mostly me, when necessary.

I was often careless, sometimes reckless, ignoring my mother's pleas of "look where you are going." Since I had a gift for falling and injuring myself to the extent that, while other mothers kept diaries of their children's achievements, my mother kept a diary of my falls and bruises. The worst example of this occurred when a washing machine and dryer were installed in a room next to the kitchen. Because I wanted the shirt I was wearing to be among the first items mother loaded into the washer, I pulled it over my head, blocking my vision, and ran toward the washer. Meanwhile, I did not know that my mother was baking a pie and had momentarily opened the oven door and left the room for a moment. In that short time, I tripped and fell flat on the surface of the open oven door, incurring severe second-degree burns on my stomach and, as a result, an ambulance ride to the hospital. The burns left scars that gradually disappeared in my late teens. From then on until now, I dutifully look where I am going.

Our Sunday adventures included pony rides at the stables in Griffith Park and long drives into the surrounding countryside in which my father invariably got us lost because he refused to use a map or ask for directions. It may sound strange, but one of my favorite stops was at Forest Lawn Memorial Park cemetery, the world's largest, to feed stale bread to the ducks in the large lake there, far away from the gravesites. We also visited our friends and relatives, including older Armenian people. Although most of these people were not related by blood, they helped to form a large family with whom my parents kept in close touch.

I remember going to Pasadena in 1947 to see the Freedom Train—a sleek, long white train with red and blue strips running horizontally on its sides—which was making a cross-country tour to give citizens the opportunity to see some of the precious documents that helped to establish our country. These included copies of the Magna Carta, Jefferson's draft of the Declaration of Independence, Lincoln's Gettysburg Address and Emancipation Proclamation. I made a report about it to my classmates. Another visit was to see Queen Mary's Doll House, the largest and most famous doll house in the world, built between 1921 and 1924 for the English Queen Mary by the great British architect Sir Edwin Lutyens. It was displayed in an unoccupied store, where we had to line up for more than an hour to get into the exhibition. While I'm sure my sister enjoyed it more than I did, I was impressed by the architecture and design, and later not only studied the work of Lutyens when I was in architecture classes and toured all the major Luytens buildings when I was in

England. This doll house is now on display at Windsor Castle in London.

On other weekends, we visited the Los Angeles County Art Museum, the Griffith Park Zoo, the Ringling Brothers Circus, which yearly pitched its huge tent in Glendale, the beaches at Santa Monica, and—my favorite—a trout pond up in the mountains stocked so fully that every child automatically caught a fish. A friend of my father's owned a dairy farm in the San Fernando Valley, and sometimes, we would drive out there for a visit. I got to milk a cow and drink its fresh, warm milk. However, there was a creepy farmhand who, in showing me how the windmill brought up water for the well, also pulled down his pants, exposing himself. I ran like hell to get out of there, and Papa never took me back to that farm again. During Christmas, we went to the parade on Hollywood Boulevard, featuring movie stars along with Santa Claus, and on New Year's Day, we saw the Pasadena Rose Parade from the roof of Grampa Pashgian's rug store. Although the Pashgian family, whose members helped to establish the parade tradition, have been long dispersed, the parade goes on.

My father was an avid fan of the radio programs of the day, particularly the live Saturday matinee broadcasts from the Metropolitan Opera in New York City. For less serious listening, but nonetheless first-rate, he regularly took me to Hollywood to be in the audience for the Sunday afternoon live broadcasts of two of the most popular programs: The Jack Benny Program, on NBC until 1949, and The Baby Snooks Show on CBS, starring comedian Fanny Brice, who was forty years older than the character she played. Both programs were broadcast in the late afternoon or early evening. Young readers may not know that Benny was one of the greatest comics of the time or that Barbra Streisand played Brice in the Broadway production of Funny Girl as well as the movie adaptation. The usual format of Benny's show—in which he played a caricature of himself as a penny-pinching man—included Benny cracking wonderful jokes, acting in skits with his wife Mary Livingstone, and his sidekick Rochester (played by Eddie Anderson, the first black man to have a recurring role in national radio and later television shows), as well as joking with the famous movie stars who made guest appearances. By contrast, the Baby Snooks Show featured a character that Fanny Brice had introduced in a 1912 vaudeville show. It was one of the nation's favorite programs and one of the first situation comedies. Sitting in the audience so close to these wonderful performers, lined up across the stage, each with his or her microphone, was for me not only a special treat, but also a memorable insight into radio broadcasting and show business in general.

Overall, my parents were generous in providing me with wonderful experiences that introduced me to the larger world. I am grateful to them, and while I could sometimes be a naughty child, I was nevertheless a happy one. Now, I am ready for the next challenge: school.

Eugene Field Elementary School (Grades Kindergarten through 6)

My first contact with education outside the home began in 1942 at the Tiny Tots School of Music when I was 4 years old and where I learned about music from the talented teacher, Miss Jackson. It was a half-day school, including lunch, after which my mother walked me home for nap time. But my official education in the Glendale Unified School District began at Eugene Field Elementary School, named for an American poet whose work was said to be especially popular with children. We were never exposed to his work, and I never knew anyone who had heard of him. Nevertheless, the school was housed in a Spanish-style building built on one-floor that ran the length of a long block so that every classroom and office had a view of Central Avenue in the front or the large playing field behind. The principal, Dr. Joseph Gannon, was a rarity at that time because he held a doctoral degree in elementary education, ran the school on the most progressive principles, and, most surprising of all, was a man in a women's world. This was partly a result of the male teachers being inducted into wartime service and partly because women teachers were preferred for the early grades.

I was enrolled in the kindergarten class in 1943 at age 4-1/2 among the few students permitted to begin at this early age. The other students were 5-7. The law that enabled this was soon changed to a five-year starting date. My teacher, Miss Jones understood that I was the baby in the class and helped me to develop some socializing skills with those older students. In the following years, my teachers left such an impression that I still recall their names and almost everything about them. Our report cards contained our academic progress and behavior. Mine routinely indicated that my academic record was excellent, but though I was generally well-behaved, I did not "avoid needless conversation," an almost Victorian-sounding neglect. The penalty for talking too much in the classroom was to order the student to stand in the corner of the room or in the adjacent "cloakroom." I don't remember anyone in the school ever wearing a cloak.

Around this time, my mother took me to my first movie, Walt Disney's Bambi (1942), which remains as moving and as beautiful today as it was when I saw it. The one thing that has stayed with me, as with many viewers my age, is the scene of Bambi's mother being shot and killed by a hunter. Although the film was part of an effort to encourage the preservation of wildlands and wildlife, some of us saw it in personal terms in which Bambi's mother became our mothers. It was too scary for me, and I ran out of the theater crying. I was not alone in that reaction. Little did I know then that the movies would occupy a major place in my later life.

Miss Sterling, my first-grade teacher, and Mr. Gannon, the principal, knew that I had scored reading and comprehension skills far above the norm on the statewide examination. Together, they convinced my parents that before the next school year, I should be "skipped" to the third grade. In those days, no one seemed to have thought about the emotional and psychological toll that such a move would have on a student. My parents accepted the move, and Gannon encouraged them not to worry but to be proud of their so-called prodigy. I got along well enough with my older classmates, some of whom became good friends through high school. Nonetheless, I knew I was different, not just in age.

So at age 6, I was skipped and occasionally required to stay after school for special tutoring so that I could catch up with the arithmetic and grammar that I would have missed in the first two grades. On other days, when I left the building with the other students for the walk home, I was sometimes harmlessly bullied by girls, not boys, who were too busy with after-school sports to pay attention to me. I wanted to play ball with them, but I was too young and too small to be of any use on a baseball or football team. The leader of the girls' group was Mary Scott (not her real name), a classmate who waited with other girls behind some bushes until I passed by. Then they jumped me, pulled me to the ground, sat on my chest and legs, and taunted me, not maliciously, but just enough to let me know who was boss. I was too small to fight back, and so endured the humiliation.

My third-grade teacher, Mrs. Austin, stood out among her colleagues, for, in contrast to the other teachers, who dressed in plain clothes, she wore chic tailored suits and jewelry. Her hair was dyed jet black. Nevertheless, teaching came first. I won her heart by operating the slide projector for her and tending to the tarantula spider that she kept in a glass case for science lessons.

During this time, there is one vivid picture I shall never forget: seeing my parents weep at the news of President Roosevelt's death in

April 1945. They were Democrats to the core and believed deeply in FDR's policies. They explained to me the significance of his death and its effect on our nation and the world, but I worried for them and myself, feeling that I was now a big ..boy because they had told me such adult news.

I entered the 4th grade in 1946. The teacher, Mrs. Bennie Greenland, was tall, thin, and stiff, the stereotypical no-nonsense New England schoolmarm depicted in some movies. She was passionate about poetry, especially the English Romantic and Victorian periods, and trained us in memorizing and reciting poems to the class. I was assigned to read a poem by Leigh Hunt, which began, as I shall never forget, with these lines: "Abou Ben Adhem (may his tribe increase!) / Awoke one night from a deep dream of peace, / And saw, within the moonlight in his room, / Making it rich, and like a lily in bloom" and so on for nine more lines. Although I got through the recitation, I believed that Mrs. Greenland had a special dislike for me. For example, I had a head of curly brown hair, and one day, to show her aloofness, she put two fingers together and, snatching a lock of my hair, said so that everyone in the room could hear: "Are you a girl or a boy?" Since I didn't know if that was a dig or a compliment, I just replied, "Boy," and she let go and theatrically wiped her fingers on a towel, suggesting that my hair needed washing. Despite things like this, I learned a great deal from her and, obviously, never forgot her. Seriously though, I've always wondered if that remark about my gender meant something that I didn't kno.w. The subject of gender identity did not become an issue in schools and society for decades.

In any event, I have never considered being anything but a male. Looking back, it seems that she was being unprofessional to humiliate an eight-year-old boy in front of his classmates.

The 5th and 6th years at Field were academic and social heaven, the result of the way in which Miss Lula Drake, a deeply dedicated instructor, went beyond normal teaching to nurture her students. For a short period of time, Miss Drake was replaced by a substitute teacher, Miss Isaline M. Yule, who took all the fun and joy out of the word learning, as it was encouraged by Miss Drake. She was a disciplinarian, a serious teacher with a formidable presence, hefty, with a noticeable black mustache, and who dressed in what were called mannish clothes. I knew that I talked too much in class—generally, it had to do with what we were studying—so one day, she called me up to her desk, scolded me in front of the class, and then ordered me to crawl under the desk and sit there. It was humiliating and caused whispering among the other students. Getting into what is called the keyhole" of the desk was a tight squeeze, with her two large legs on either side of me and, unbeknownst to her, a direct view up her skirt. It was Christmas time, so she let me come out from under to join a classroom party. I could never forget Isaline M. Yule or stop wondering what the "M" stood for.

Soon, Miss Drake returned to the classroom, older than Miss Sterling, far less chic than Miss Austin, and not menacing like Miss Yule. I loved her so much that I couldn't wait to get to school each day. She nurtured my love of learning, and strengths and weaknesses, and spent considerable time enhancing the former. She knew I loved to read and recommended books that I could borrow from the Glendale Public Library. Soon, I received an award from the library for being the student who borrowed the most books in one year. Predictably, I did average work in arithmetic and science lessons but enjoyed most the one day each month when the art and music teacher visited our classroom. This person was an all-purpose expert in both arts and helped us with singing, discussing reproductions of paintings, and playing simple instruments like the autoharp. Amid all this enlightenment, I also had my first awareness of puberty.

Miss Drake was supportive in her mentorship, helping me to cross the scary chasm between elementary and junior high school, which I would enter at age eleven. She assigned special reports more challenging than those assigned to the other students and held me back after class was over (it was the last class of the day) to show me objects or talk about things that might interest me. She impacted my life so much that I kept in touch with her through my college years.

By the age of six or seven, I had already been reading books far above what the local library suggested for my age category, and the librarians became my mentors and friends, eagerly moving me out of "children's books" into the "young adult" offerings: novels by Robert Louis Stevenson, travel adventures by Richard Halliburton, poetry by Longfellow and Tennyson and other poets that would continue to be the only poetry I knew until I got to college. Poetry was somehow overlooked in high school and replaced by the safest and dreariest of required books, such as Sir Walter Scott's Ivanhoe. I systematically started to educate myself, and by thirteen, I had read plays by George

Bernard Shaw and Eugene O'Neill and novels by John Steinbeck, F. Scott Fitzgerald, and Willa Cather. Add to that the plays and stories of William Saroyan, a fellow Armenian who was our sometime guest for dinner, and various other writers, and you can see the literary nourishment I craved.

We received The New Yorker at home, and I devoured it weekly, along with the seemingly endless supply of the condensed books one could read in the Readers' Digest. My parents supported this regimen heartily, checking books out of the library that were considered too old for me or purchasing them when necessary. All the aunts and uncles in our extended family knew what to give me for Christmas and birthdays: books, books, and more books, often hardbacks or presentation copies. I was allowed to see films at the local theaters, selected by my mother, and preferred two disparate genres: westerns and musicals, both of which were considered safe for young people to see. On any Saturday, and for a quarter, we would spend hours enjoying two features, several cartoons, a newsreel, and a travelogue. The theaters were deemed to be safe for young children, and it was a good place for parents to park us while they did serious shopping or just enjoyed themselves for a few hours in a quiet house.

You might think that such literary precociousness would attract the attention of teachers who would take me under their wing and encourage my love of learning. Just the opposite. With the notable exception of Miss Drake, who was an elementary school teacher, it got me nowhere in junior high and high school, particularly when I would raise my hand and mention a writer or book that no one in the room, often including the teacher, had read. I wasn't showing off, but I'm sure it seemed that way. Most of my fellow students did not savor reading as I did. I don't blame the teachers, for they were typical of that period in American history: simple and uncontroversial women, usually single, and a few married men who liked the schedule, security, and status that came with the job. They were college graduates who had probably taken courses in education. Some of them were genuinely inspired in the classroom; others cared more about discipline than subject matter. Nevertheless, they all had their strengths and weaknesses, in all these years and through high school, I don't remember a single bad teacher. At that time, I would never have dreamed that I would spend a major part of my career as a college professor.

When the United States entered World War II, I was 3 years old and 7 when it ended. Through it all, children of my age began to mature faster than previously because they were given responsibilities that they would not have earlier. My responsibilities were helping mother around the house, caring for and feeding the chickens, enduring the frequent blackouts—my father saying, "get under that table. Roosevelt says to get under, so do it."—and learning to adjust to the food rationing that made such a difference in what we ate. And it wasn't just food, for gasoline was also rationed and in short supply. We could not easily go out on our usual Sunday trips. Once a month Uncle Harry (who was Ida's husband and not my uncle at all but called that because he was a Barsam) paid us a visit. He owned a grocery store and was able to bring us food, particularly such precious things like butter, when our ration book stamps were used up. We were always well fed, for my mother had preserved jars of tomatoes, peaches, and other fruits. One day a neighbor who happened to glimpse down the staircase to the cellar and see the jars all lined up, accused my mother of being a hoarder. She was nothing of the kind, just a very practical housewife planning and using her home-canned fruits and vegetables to feed her family. Another uncle named Matthew Jamgochian was a delightful man who had built a large playhouse for his three children. When his children grew too old to use the playhouse, he took it apart and reassembled it in our backyard. It was a charming house, perhaps 12' W x 12' D x 9' H, painted White, with large windows on all sides, one that was big enough for several children to enjoy and for adults to enter and keep an eye on them. During the war, with everyone's concern about food, it also served as a henhouse for raising chickens. It was my chore to feed and water them, which I took seriously, but I was upset to see them later at the dinner table. For the war effort, I also tended the backyard victory garden that provided us with fresh vegetables.

Cub Scouts and YMCA Summer Camp

At the age of nine, I joined the Cub Scouts, and my mother volunteered to be the den mother. Ten boys met in the backyard of our Pacific Avenue house, and however busy we may have been, the only activity I remember now was roasting potatoes on an open fire and eating them, drowned in butter, as a treat. After that dinner, we pitched our pup tents on the lawn and spent the night. The simple act of sleeping alone in a tent outside was a challenge, the sort of thing that helped me to gain self-confidence by playing and working with other boys. After we moved to the new house on Matilija Road, my parents enrolled me in swimming and boxing classes at the YMCA and encouraged me to go to the Y summer camp. Thus, I made my first solo trip in the summer of my tenth year. This was not only a challenge but a treat for me because Camp Fox was located on Santa Catalina Island, some twenty-seven miles off the California coast, far away from home. Catalina is a private island still owned by members of the Wrigley gum family, and in those days, only a small portion was occupied by outsiders. The rest were day trippers to Avalon, the only city. Far away, Cat Harbor at the Isthmus was the site of much Hollywood filming. There were two Y camps, the other being Camp Orizaba, operated by the Pasadena YMCA. Today, the Catalina Island Conservancy manages the botanical gardens, wilderness areas, and wildlife sanctuaries; nonetheless, unmonitored public access to much of the island remains restricted. However, while Camp Fox still operates, Camp Orizaba does not.

In order to get there, we boarded a bus that took us from Glendale to San Pedro harbor, then embarked on the water taxis that would take us to the camp, where the usual stay for each boy was seven nights. The Catalina Channel is noted as one of the seven deadliest bodies of water in the world, no wonder given that its heavy waves tossed the boat so much that we were all seasick, but eventually, we got there. Camp Fox was a safe enclave, accessible only by boat and only to the campers, the staff, and occasional merchants who delivered provisions. Unlike some other summer camps, parents were not permitted to visit their sons on Catalina Island, because getting to and from there was not easy. The only communication with the outside world was by mail or the two-way radio, used only in emergencies. The camp covered many acres, surrounded on three sides by formidable mountains and by a placid bay on the fourth. For most of us, this was the first extended trip away from home without family, and most of us enjoyed the freedom. Of course, I missed my mother, father, and sister, so, like most campers, I corresponded with them by mail almost daily. And because my mother was a good correspondent, I generally received a letter when we heard "mail call," but some boys went back to their tent and moped because no one had written to them that day.

Campers were housed in large tents with wooden floors raised about two feet above the ground as protection from creepy-crawly things, like lizards and even snakes. Instead of glass, the windows were covered by screens to keep out the mosquitoes and other bugs. We slept in sleeping bags on bunk beds, and anyone not making up his bed neatly every morning paid a penalty, usually some grim chore in the kitchen. A counselor, usually a young man in his teens, also slept in the tent. His job was to keep us quiet, not fighting with one another, and encouraging us to practice the values that the camp taught us. Also, since toilets were located quite a distance away from the tents, which meant a long walk in the dark, he accompanied any boy who needed to go during the night. The reason for this was to scare away from the camp the deadly wild boars that roamed over the island, yet in all my years of going to Camp Fox, I saw only one boar, and that was in broad daylight. It was no surprise that the meals served cafeteria style did not equal the food that we were used to at home. However, accepting new and different situations was one of the things that made the summer camp experience so important to growing up.

In an ordinary week, the summer weather was clear and sunny and filled with activities, including swimming, water skiing, hiking, crafts work, and, at night, sitting around the fire pit with the tent leaders. At those sessions, we listened to inspirational stories, sang folk songs as well as hymns, and then said prayers before going off to our tents to sleep. The religious component was consistent with the YMCA's goal at that time to infuse us with Christian values. Today, the YMCA and YWCA are known simply as the Y, with membership open to everyone regardless of faith.

I enjoyed my first visit so much that I returned to the camp for the next few summers, each time being given more responsibility with chores, so at fourteen and in my first year in high school, I was asked to return that summer as a tent counselor. I knew what I was getting into, for I had watched the counselors for years, but we were given only rudimentary training. Nevertheless, I believed I could fulfill the expectations. I worked through the full summer, helping several different groups of campers to enjoy themselves. And I enjoyed myself, having lots of free time and sitting with the other tent counselors at meals. I particularly enjoyed water skiing.

Some background is needed for what you'll read next. As noted earlier, my first cousin by marriage, Bill Graf, was a film producer in

Hollywood. When working on The African Queen, he and the star, Humphrey Bogart, became friends. Bogie was the master of his sailboat Santana, and almost every weekend in the summer months, he and his wife Lauren Bacall sailed in the Catalina Channel. Most of the other weekend sailors, including other Hollywood personalities, laid anchor at Cat Harbor at the Isthmus, where there were a few restaurants and a food market. It was isolated and tourists were few, but Bogie preferred the calm bay in front of Camp Fox for a safe overnight harbor, free from others.

One day, water skiing in unusually rough waters, I was too busy to notice that the usual sharks were nearby, diving and playing. They can still be deadly, and you shouldn't second guess them. Some of our campers, who were out fishing, saw them, called out to warn me. But the sharks were closer than I thought, and seeing Bogart's boat nearby, I yelled at the man driving my towboat to get me there for safety. When we got close enough for me to swim to the yacht, I grabbed its rope ladder, ignored the sign that said "No Entry," and climbed up onto the deck. At last, I was safe and called out, "Hello, hello." Bacall appeared from the lower deck. Taking one look at one very scared boy, she brought blankets to wrap me. I apologized for disobeying the "no entry" sign and reminded her that we had met once before in the company of Bill and Betty Graf. "Oh," she said, "then you must be Dickie," a name I'd outlived by then. Presently, Bogie (he was always called that) himself stuck his head out and, assessing the scene, called for a crew member to "bring hot chocolate for the kid."

Fortified by that, I stopped shaking and tried to appear mature, but that lovely couple understood how frightened I was and did everything possible to make me feel safe, including an invitation to join them for a very nice lunch. Bacall wanted to phone my parents and tell them what happened, but I begged her not to, and I never told them until some years later. No need to worry them when everything turned out alright. Finally, a member of the Santana's crew rowed me to shore only to face a barrage of questions about the Bogarts and their boat.

That summer was the last I was to spend at Camp Fox. Tent Counsellors earned different colored neck scarves for their achievements, and I did very well for myself. But now, I was fourteen and ready to enter high school. I have satisfying memories of the summers I spent at the camp, especially as a counselor. I learned leadership skills that served me well in the forthcoming years, both in high school, college, and my teaching career. And so, with my moving on into an older and more diverse world, I was fortunate to meet important people in many fields, sometimes when planned and sometimes just out of the deep blue sea. But Humphrey Bogart and Lauren Bacall were the only ones to be introduced by a shark.

Chapter Four:
Junior High School

1949-1951

In 1949, we moved from 1013 Pacific Avenue to a new house at 1001 Matilija (ma-til-a-ha) Road, close to the foothills of the Verdugo Mountains, a mile and a quarter walk to the school. The house was built in the Mediterranean-Spanish style on one-half acre of land. The ground floor was dominated by a 40' x 25' living room whose ceiling was supported by redwood beams that had been hand-stenciled in color with ancient Mexican designs. A large fireplace dominated one end of the room; on one long wall, double doors led to a small, private patio; on the other side of the room, a large window afforded a view across the lawn (which I mowed weekly) to neighbors' houses on Matilija Road. Continuing the tour, the ground floor included a dining room, kitchen, laundry room, and breakfast room. What was originally intended as a servant's room and bath was assigned as my quarters. On the second floor, there were bedrooms for my parents and sister and a bathroom whose walls were covered in yellow and black tiles. The back garden had two avocado trees, an orange tree, and lots of shrubbery and flowers. It also had a rose garden that was soon to play a major role in my life. This was the perfect Southern California house, and to me, it was the most beautiful house in the world.

At night, however, the surroundings were very dark. Large trees arched over the streets, forming a closed canopy, and the only lighting was a single bare bulb of low wattage on one corner only. Since the blocks were unusually long, those feeble lights were useless, making the neighborhood seem isolated and possibly dangerous. This made it a magnet for prowlers, people who found safety in the darkness as they moved from garden to garden, looking for open windows or unlocked doors. It was just such a prowler who, from an outside patio, opened the unlocked door of my bedroom one night and got one foot through the door. Screaming for my father, I ran upstairs to his bedroom, and the man escaped. The police came, and I gave them a description of the thief, but they never found him. My father calmed me down with a promise to build a bedroom for me on a terrace upstairs. He already had the specifications in his head: knotty pine walls, built-in furniture including a single bed, desk, dresser, and bookcases. It took about one year to build before I could move. In the meantime, he had already employed a security service to check the property twice each night to ensure all doors and ground-floor windows were locked. Such a service was customary with most houses in the neighborhood.

As a young man, my father wanted to be an architect, but circumstances, as we have seen, foiled that ambition. However, it did not dampen his interest. Before we moved to Matilija Road, he had already designed the plans for a new house to be built on the property we owned on Kenneth Road. However, my mother wished to live above Kenneth Road, not just on it, and while the construction of the new house proceeded, she found the house of her dreams on Matilija Road, two very long blocks above Kenneth. We all agreed that the house was for us. When Dad completed construction on his house, he immediately sold it.

Toll Junior High School

In the Fall of 1959, I started in the 7th-grade class at Eleanor J. Toll Junior High School, grades 7-9, now known as E.J. Toll Middle School. It was named for Mrs. Toll, the grandmother of a wealthy Glendale family who took a special interest in education. On the first day, I realized that I was now in a new academic and social world. The administration there consisted of the principal, a German-born woman named Miss Joanna Heideman, and two vice-principals, one for girls, the other for boys. Miss Heideman was a tall, imposing figure, authoritative, humorless, and a little frightening to me. She spoke with a thick German accent at a time, just after World War II, when Germans were not very popular. She was not popular with students, and during our gym period in a far-off corner of the playing field, away from the eyes of the school's leader, we had fun mocking her by rolling up our tee shirts to resemble a bra and doing a jig we called the Joanna. We were clearly a unique group of boys.

Joanna's vice-principals were equally stern in their authority. Being called into their offices was serious business, at least to them, and often resulted in a phone call to parents. If you were summoned, they might have had an academic matter to discuss, but primarily, it was your behavior that motivated them. The boy's vice principal called my mother several times because my Collie dog named Lucky had escaped from our yard and arrived in front of the school, quite a trip for it was more than a mile away. He sat at the school's front door, barking to get attention, the sound easily reaching Joanna's office. My mother, embarrassed and apologetic, was asked to pick up the dog and take him home. While she liked cats, she didn't like Lucky, who further alienated her by digging up flowers and other plants. In the end, Lucky wasn't so lucky. She told me that she could no longer tolerate his misbehaving and gave him to a family that wanted a dog. Later that evening, I learned the truth, that she had him euthanized, a cruel act just to save some flowers. Yes, she lied to me, perhaps to protect my feelings, but she must have known that I would find out what really happened to my dog.

Toll was a serious school where we received three years of a sound education in language, history, mathematics, foreign languages, and science. I especially looked forward to English classes with Mr. David Leek, a humble man who frequently reminded us that he was born in Minnesota in a sod house. At our age, he had limited educational opportunities and reminded us to value our education and do our best. He soon became a mentor and encouraged my writing. I had no idea then that I would earn a doctoral degree in English literature, teach in that field, and write books of my own. I have a lasting memory of Mr. Leek himself bending over me to correct a grammatical error when a blob of wax fell from one of his ears onto my essay, and we both burst into laughter. I kept in touch with him through college. He died before my first book was published in 1973, and I would have been very proud to send him a copy.

At Toll, I joined the student orchestra and learned to play the violin. The instructor and conductor, Mrs. Myrtle Exner, was very serious about music and generally made us enthusiastic also. We learned many classical works, albeit those suitable to teenage musicians, and she demanded the most of our abilities. In addition to the violin, she taught me to play the viola. She was very sensitive and emotional and could burst into tears when she was unhappy with our playing. I felt sorry for her. Our year-end concert, attended by fellow students and, of course, proud parents, was taken very seriously by all involved. To show her appreciation for the conductor's efforts, each year, my mother made a corsage of camellias from her garden for Mrs. Exner to wear on the conductor's podium.

Physical education at Toll was a different world from the music room. It was conducted in what seemed to me an almost militaristic manner, with the coaches bullying and yelling at us. Boys were required to buy gym clothes, consisting of a t-shirt, gym shorts, a jockstrap, socks, and tennis shoes. To acquire these items, my mother took me to Glendale Sporting Goods, but when it came to the jockstrap, she told the clerk to choose a small one because, as she said, "he doesn't have anything to put in it." She was too dignified a woman to say something like that in public, but she did, and it embarrassed me. This wasn't the first time she tried to humiliate me. I still don't know if she thought that her comment was funny or if she wanted to continue her habit of degrading me, such as telling me to "be a man" and go out and play baseball rather than sit at home and read. I had another reason to worry about the jock strap, for although I could be proud of my well-formed body, I was born with one undescended testicle and sensitive about being naked in front of the other boys. And, as for being men, do not forget, we were still boys in various stages of puberty.

Sons are supposed to love their mothers, but her behavior was going in a very dangerous direction. She was sick, obsessed with the idea that something was wrong with me. I was too young for such behavior and have never forgotten, let alone forgiven. It muddied the already complicated waters of puberty and created an inner conflict within me about masculinity that I then failed to comprehend. She could not understand or explain this psychological abuse of me or protect me from it. What would come from these misguided efforts to make a man out of me? Why wasn't my father concerned at all with her attitude? I now understand why some sons have a love-hate relationship with their mothers.

At this time, all Toll students were going through puberty or had completed it. Thus, boys became interested in girls and vice versa, and the word sex raised all kinds of questions and answers. Along with my pals, I knew nothing about girls and did not have a crush on a girlfriend, or even a boyfriend for that matter, just good companions. As for sex, at this point, I was a pre-teenager in a town that did not openly confront the thorny issues of sex, gender, and identity. These issues were not discussed openly at school or at home. So, in the first week of the semester, we boys were seated in a classroom and given our first lesson in basic sex education. It was provided by the gym coaches. Unlike today, when many parents object to having such classes at an early age, I don't remember it being a public issue in Glendale. The lights in the room were dimmed, and we were shown Human Reproduction, a 24-minute animated film that uses detailed visuals and a serious narrator to provide the facts of human reproduction. I distinctly remember this. Naturally, some boys were bewildered by what they were learning, while others giggled and made stupid remarks, trying to show that they knew the facts of life. I recently found the film on the internet and watched its clinical explanation of how babies were born, with no attention being paid to the love that is often part of the sex act. Even if you were one of a group of boys who bragged about what they knew about sex through hearsay and gossip, this film left us with useful medical knowledge for later years. Today, however, this film would elicit howls of laughter from boys of our age who know more than we could have imagined. The girls were shown a Walt Disney animated film, The Story of Menstruation. Note the subject has nothing to do with what the boys were taught. The implicit warning in our film—don't do this until marriage was omitted in theirs. Thus, many girls were left clueless.

In gym class, after playing baseball or running track, we went to the showers, where I felt a little different from the other boys because their bodies were more mature than mine. A boy called Whitey, the tallest boy in the class, who was 18 years old and should have been in high school, had the largest penis in the group. Frank D'Angelo (not his real name), who was as short as Whitey was tall, also had a large penis, so I then realized that a boy's height has nothing to do with his penis size. Whitey bragged about getting a girl pregnant, thus forcing her to leave school. He was expelled when it was learned that he had syphilis. I had looked up the word in a dictionary, so I understood what a dangerous disease it was, but I was also amused that a prominent writer said that syphilis was one of the most beautiful-sounding words in English.

In my last summer before high school, one of my parents' friends offered me a job at California Hot Springs in the Sequoia National Forest, a resort he owned. He wanted me to oversee activities for the children as well as serve as one of the lifeguards at the swimming pool. Like Camp Fox, this would offer an opportunity to have new experiences and meet new people. The arrangement offered a good salary, bed and board, and one day off each week. I was assigned to share a cabin with Matt, who had graduated from Glendale High School and had lately gotten in trouble with heroin and spent some time in a rehab center. Officials there released him on the condition that he would spend the summer working at the resort and avoid all drugs. Despite our differences, he was a serious person, and I liked him. We arranged to have our off days together and drove around to see the sights of the national forest. When he bragged about his experience with women, I asked him to teach me how to have sex with them and got a full explanation. He also told me about having sex with a man. Matt was having a sexual relationship with one of the resort's female employees, who introduced me to a girlfriend slightly older than me and who taught me about heavy petting. When the summer was finished, we both returned to Glendale and even though I tried to reach him, I never heard from Matt again.

John Stoppard was among my best friends. His house was on the opposite end of Matilija from ours, a huge place in the Cape Cod style, and stood out among the many Spanish-style houses. It was across the street from the house of Casey Stengel, the New York Yankees manager who led the team to win the World Series championship five consecutive times (1949–1953), an achievement unique in major league baseball history. Casey and his wife Edna, who was born in Glendale, spent their winters in New York and their summers in Glendale. They were a reclusive couple but generous in letting the neighborhood kids use their tennis court and swimming pool. Since they had no children of their own to greet their return for the summer, John, his sister Jenny, my sister Sue, and several of the Stengel's nephews and nieces formed a ragtag band consisting of accordion, cymbals, flute, and drums to serenade his arrival. Standing in the Stengel's driveway as their car approached, we sang "Take Me Out of the Ballgame." After that, Casey distributed treasures for each of us: baseballs autographed by Joe DiMaggio, Phil Rizzuto, Mickey Mantle, and the other greats, photographs, and other memorabilia. I had a ball signed by the entire winning team, but when I was away at college, my mother gave it to a young relative. How was she to know the emotional value it had had for me or that in later years? Why didn't she ask me if I still wanted it? In a few years later, it would become worth thousands of dollars when people began to sell such sports memorabilia.

My junior high school education was not only a rite of passage from my childhood to puberty, for it also opened a new world of extra-curricular activities. To further my interest in theater, my parents took me to Los Angeles to see the Broadway shows on tour. That made me truly fascinated with the theater, as well as the movies, which suggested to them that I might want a career in show business. It's often said that these things are seeded when you are about ten or so. In my neighborhood, I staged modest shows in our backyard in the summer and the garage in the winter. These included scenes from familiar works as well as some very simple things I had written. My friends pitched in, making the settings and gathering old clothes for costumes. Neighbors were invited and expected to contribute 25 cents for the privilege of attending. Afterwards, my parents served drinks. It was great fun.

From this first experience, my father designed a little theater for me. It measured 4' deep and 4' high and was intended to sit on a table. There was a proscenium arch to frame the stage. The fly area above the stage, but out of sight of the audience, contained the main curtains, working space of puppet handlers, strings of Christmas lights, and some small spotlights, all on dimmers, scenery, and working space for puppets. My mother made the gold-fringed red velvet main curtain, which we opened and closed with a small electric pulley. I treasured this theater, often spending time after school, not doing my homework but creating new productions. Both my parents participated. My father's enthusiasm in creating this little theater was, I now realize, ironic, for while he seemed to be encouraging me to pursue a theatrical career, he refused to permit my mother to pursue one in the movies.

My father was generous with his understanding and love, but there were limits to his financial generosity. Not because he was a miser but because he wanted to teach me the value of money. For example, although all my boyfriends in the neighborhood had a set of electric trains, he consistently refused to buy one for me. But then, how many boys have a father who made them a theater to play with? He gave me a small weekly allowance, which I earned by mowing the front and back lawns and washing our cars. For neighbors, I also cleaned swimming pools, raked leaves, and mowed lawns. I used my bike to deliver The Los Angeles Times and the Herald Express, which proved the most lucrative of my outside work. Monthly, I would visit each subscriber and collect the $2.00 subscription rate, 50 cents of which was my fee. Yet, given that this was an affluent town, there were always people who made excuses for not having the $2.00, making it necessary for me to return to collect, sometimes more than once.

When I was fifteen, I got a job in the stock room of Harris & Frank, a men's clothing store in downtown Glendale, and within a year, I was promoted to junior salesman, a job that I continued through high school and from which I built a savings account. As for college, which was right around the corner, my father paid for my tuition with the understanding that I would use my savings to cover any personal expenses. The older I got, the more money I made, and thus, the more I understood the value of money.

When I graduated from Toll, I had finished puberty. Academically, I was ready for high school, but personally and socially, I needed to know more about sex before I began mixing with my more mature friends there. I had mastered the pleasure of masturbation and understood the changes occurring in my body, such as my voice changing. I learned how to shave, but sex in all its variations was what I really wanted to know more about.

Chapter Five: Sex Education

The sexual culture and practices of Americans have changed in many ways in the past fifty years since I was an adolescent. Then, newspaper and magazine articles involving sexual issues were not likely to cover such a topic as homosexuality. To get books about homosexuality, one had to go to the library and consult the card catalog for the few existing books on the subject. In the 1950s, men could read such notable works of fiction as Gore Vidal's The City and the Pillar (1948), James Baldwin's Giovanni's Room (1956), Truman Capote's Other Voices, and Other Rooms (1948). Lesbians could read Alice Walker's The Color Purple (1982), Virginia Woolf's Orlando (1928), or Rubyfruit Jungle (1973) by Rita Nae Brown. Excellent as they may be, they are fiction, not fact. Today, there is an abundance of non-fiction books, as well as scientific treatises and, of course, fiction. As for movies on homosexuality, Hollywood comedies in the 1930s often had a male character with very womanly behavior, but it was not until the last twenty years that the subject was treated openly and honestly in movies as well as television shows.

In the previous chapter, I described the rudimentary efforts made to educate junior high students about sex. In those days, parents were generally expected to discuss sex with their children and answer their questions. However, many parents avoided the subject and gave the task of explaining the "birds and the bees" to someone else. Of course, there were many people whose life included rich sexual experiences, but most Americans were far away from what we know and do today. As far as I could tell, my parents apparently had an abundant and happy sex life. They set aside Sunday afternoons for their pleasures and made sure that me and my sister were out of the house. Even then, rather than discuss it, they had pamphlets—one for boys and the other for girls—encouraged my sister and me to read them. As I remember, these booklets were more informative than anything I'd seen or heard before. So far, all this indoctrination suggested that sex existed only for reproduction and ignored the other pleasures and benefits of a well-informed and healthy sexual life.

I got my introduction to sex at age 11 when John Stoppard spent the night in a sleepover and taught me how to masturbate or jerk off, as we say now. On that first occasion, my climax and ejaculation were an exciting surprise. Thereafter, he and I continued to jerk off together, never making any physical contact between our bodies. It was just what boys did when they were together. In the summertime, we pitched a tent in the backyard, away from the house, and had our pleasure there. Decades later, I was reminded of that when seeing the film Brokeback Mountain, where a sexual encounter in a tent transformed one undecided man into a gay lover.

When I read in the newspaper that a high school girl, our neighbor, was raped the previous night in front of her house, I realized that sex could be violent. Going to my mother, I asked, "What is rape?" and she replied, "Wait until your father comes home and he'll tell you." And he did. In the early 1950s, I began to learn that sex wasn't just physical contact of all kinds but that there were also variations. This time, the front-page news reported Christine Jorgensen's transition from male to female. I was only seven at the time, but I read the newspaper daily and understood that this was an astonishing scientific feat. Transition is now common throughout the world. An equally complex issue is gender identity, for which a person identifies as male, female, both, or neither.

Nature or Nurture?

Nature or nurture: what makes one a homosexual? The following answer is a comic one. The playwright Edward Albee, who was gay and had a conflicted relationship with his mother, said that when he was in college, he saw written on a bathroom wall: "My mother made me gay." Beneath it, writing in another hand, was: "If I gave her the yarn, would she make me one too?" Nobody makes you gay.

We still do not have an adequate understanding of the biological and social sources of homosexuality. This is not the place for weighing all the issues concerned with what makes us what we are, but it's enough to say that I believe that I was born bisexual. I have a history of satisfactory sexual relations with both men and women, with, eventually, a stronger preference for men. After I met the man who became my partner of nearly forty years—from 1977 until his death in 2016—I did not have sex with a woman again. And today, my old age renders sexual contact impossible.

At 14, I had my first sex experience with an adult male. It happened this way. The Glendale Centre Theatre was casting for a production of "Cheaper by the Dozen," a Broadway hit that was popular with community theaters for its wholesome content and good humor. Although I had no previous experience in acting, I auditioned and won the minor role of Joe Scales, a school cheerleader, giving me five minutes on stage to deliver my lines. The director, Hugh Johnson, a television director in his day job, helped make my short performance a success with the audience. Hugh was ten years older, and during the weeks we performed, one thing led to another, and one afternoon, I found myself in his apartment and bed. Neither of us considered that seducing a minor was a dangerous business, and we met a few times more until my mother got suspicious of my frequent trips to his apartment, and I voluntarily stopped seeing him. Some five years later, I visited him and saw that he had been drinking heavily. He said he felt guilty for initiating me into sex and that it had made him an alcoholic. Although I never saw him again, a few years later, I began to see in the larger world a very frequent link between alcoholism and homosexuality. However, I would not have had another homosexual experience until I started college.

While in high school, I enjoyed being with girls at a dance or the movies but did not attempt to have sex with them. Petting, yes, but sex, no. I felt that it was too dangerous to try. Teenagers can screw up their whole lives by not knowing about protection, and there were few stories of our fellow students getting pregnant and leaving school in shame. But boys will be boys, and we spent a lot of time talking about sex. Those who had experienced some sexual activity with a girl said that it could be awkward after a dance, in the front seat of a car, touching her breasts through her clothes, and wrestling with the fasteners on a formidable array of garments they wore then (dress or blouse, slip or camisole, and bra) that made their efforts difficult, but not impossible.

At the time, I was going steady with a girl I very much liked, and while we did a lot of heavy petting, nothing else occurred until we continued the relationship in college. Then, after a fraternity party, we drove to the beach and enjoyed our first sex encounter on a blanket. We remained very much a couple throughout the sophomore year; she wore my fraternity pin, which was then like being engaged. But since I had begun to have sex with men, I had to be honest with her, and we broke up. That did not stop me from continuing to date women and have sex with some of them, but it was safe sex, not love.

I was in a quandary. What did I think about females? Some of my best friends, then as now, were women. And, as I write in my 86th year, I frequently enjoy an evening out with one of them. But in high school, my attitude toward girls was mixed. While I had a certain puritanical streak and regarded women as pure—men were never pure in my view—that was balanced by an imaginative sexual desire for both females and males. I tended to date the virtuous girls, where the goodnight kiss after an evening was acceptable, but nothing more. feared going further with a girl, even with protection. My libido was willing, but my intellect was stronger.

During high school, my father paid scant attention to my dating girls. However, my mother insisted that I spend equal amounts of time with both girls and boys. Because I spent much time with books, she would urge me to go out and play baseball with the boys, accompanied by the humiliating remark, "Be a man, like your father!" Homosexuality was not an option for me in high school, and my mother never mentioned the subject; she probably thought, like many people, that it was only a "phase" that boys outgrew.

I never heard the word gay until college and had no idea of how many of my fellow students were gay, if only because so many were still in the closet. We were a little older then and could make such decisions without parental knowledge. One of my fraternity brothers and I had sex occasionally in his apartment. I also had an affair with the son of a movie star. Today, however, at most colleges, gays are out and free to be what they are; gay organizations are a political force; and classes on all aspects of sexuality are regular parts of the curriculum.

The phrase coming out, which is now universally known, was used in the late 19th and early 20th century to refer to debutantes who came out at grand society balls, an indication that they were eligible for marriage. From the 1930s to the 1950s, that remained the prevailing usage of the term. Even in the 1950s, people were vague, saying that a person was "a friend of Dorothy's" or "one of the of the club" to identify someone they thought, hoped, or knew was gay. So, it was not until the Gay Rights Movement got into full swing in the 1970s that one began to hear free and open usage of the word gay and the term coming out. The Gay Pride parades were coming out events, public and theatrical, with gays taking over major cities to celebrate their gayness. For the first time, movies and TV shows offered stories in which gay people were portrayed seriously and not as subjects of hatred. The AIDS crisis changed everything in the gay world, killing some 50 million people and significantly delaying the implementation of gay rights. Subsequently, there has been meaningful progress guaranteeing gay rights as well as making them a welcome part of many levels of our society. The multi-purpose acronym LGBTQIA represents the world of Lesbian, Gay, Bisexual, Transgender, Queer, Intersex, and Asexual people. Gay issues are frequent in the daily media. All of this has made it easier and less painful to come out to one's parents, coworkers, classmates, and friends, and it represents a major step in establishing one's identity. Still, for some people, it is easy, for others, it is difficult.

To include gay issues in our everyday discourse not only removes the stigma and fear that prevailed in times past but also encourages people to declare themselves as gay. Of course, that was not always the situation. When I was in college in the 1950s and 1960s, the California law forbade being an open, active homosexual. Plainclothes cops frequented gay bars, eager to arrest anyone they could entrap. Gay people were outsiders, fearful of our thoughts, words, hopes, and actions. Today, there remain pockets of gay hatred in cities where primitive attitudes and laws remain in force, but we are mostly to declare our pride.

Remember that this is an account of my life in the 1960s when I discovered sex in different situations but was not ready to come out openly. It was not until graduate school that I found the right occasion to do that, or it found me.

Chapter Six:
Neighborhood Life

Before we get to my high school years, here's what was happening in my life outside of school, at home, in our neighborhood, and in other locations. Some incidents are forgotten, but other moments remain in my memory. For one thing, I was close to the kids in my neighborhood, both girls and boys, who were always ready to do things together. For example, we'd go into the mountains on the Brand estate, a risky thing to do because of the rattlesnakes there. For protection, we carried our BB or pellet guns and could easily kill them if necessary. One snake that we killed had a large round swelling in its body, and we assumed it was a rat or some other small animal that it had swallowed. However, we were curious enough to bring it to Mr. Donald Coleman, our biology teacher who lived in the neighborhood. He took a pen knife and cut the snake open. It wasn't a rat, just an intact orange, which Mr. Coleman cut open with his knife and ate. I knew he was a little weird, but that was disgusting.

Across from the Coleman's house was what we called the haunted house. It was an empty, perfect place, inside and out, but it had been mysteriously unoccupied for years. Although there was a For Sale sign, no one seemed interested. So, we found a way to get into the house without causing any damage. We would take food with us and have picnics on the floor. Because we left it as we found it, we were never discovered.

The house next to ours was occupied by the Boger family, consisting of a very old woman and her grown, unmarried daughter and son. If you went on their property and rang the doorbell—for example, soliciting for some charity or school event—Mrs. Boger would come out and threaten you with a heavy stick. She was clearly crazy, as is evidenced by the following. On the far side of her property was Dr. Roberts' large estate with its horse-riding track circling the property and passing closely to the Boger's' property. The doctor kept a horse on this property for his morning ride. Mrs. Boger didn't like that, and one morning, she leaned out of her second-story window as he was galloping past and struck him on the head with a heavy piece of wood. He fell from the horse, suffering a concussion but no broken bones. I really don't remember if he took legal action against her, but the Roberts family moved out within a short period.

After the old woman died, the son moved away, but her daughter tried to become friendly with neighbors. However, if you asked her questions about her mother or the reason for their isolated life, she would change the subject. Eventually, she got married, sold the house, and moved away, but the Boger family remained a neighborhood mystery like the haunted house.

Life at Home

Food was a particularly important part of our family life at home. We all ate breakfast at different times, and my mother packed brown bag lunches for me. Not just any lunch, but (and I say this with some sarcasm) a true vegetarian delight: a wedge of cabbage, carrot and celery sticks, a hard-boiled egg, or some slight variation, and for dessert, always a little box of raisins. I realize now that my mother was years ahead by stressing such healthy and politically correct food, but this was decades before vegetarianism became popular, and it certainly set me apart from my fellow students. No one ever wanted to exchange their slice of chocolate cake for a box of raisins. After I was in high school, I ate in the cafeteria, for social, not food, reasons.

At home, the four of us regarded dinner seriously and ate together happily. Indeed, we looked forward to dinner because my mother was a great cook. Satisfying my father's preference for Armenian meals was her first concern, but she had mastered a wide range of recipes and also respected her children's likes and dislikes. She also knew instinctively how to use food to soothe our quarreling or to coax us to come down to dinner when we were sulking in our rooms. We were expected to stay at the table until my father said we could go.

In addition to cooking, Mother was a talented hostess. The Armenians who formed our larger outside family—those aunts and uncles I've mentioned—were at our house far more than we were ever at theirs. It was a clan with its own regulations. Some of them did not cook themselves and were unable to entertain. Nevertheless, showing their appreciation for her hospitality, some brought liquor, flowers, or chocolates. Others reciprocated more formally. For example, we often entertained three siblings: two brothers and a sister who lived together with their elderly mother and never married. They were wealthy, had a full-time cook, and invited us to their house once a year at Christmas time, but not for a meal. Tea, drinks, and presents were a good substitute. All of this was taken in stride.

My Mother made sure that I understood proper social behavior. During these frequent evenings, and before I left for college, I learned a lot about entertaining and being entertained. Also, I learned the importance of taking gifts to hostesses, sending thank you notes, and reciprocating when, later, I could ask people to dinner at my apartment. I was a specialist in properly setting a table for a large dinner party. On Easter, Thanksgiving, and Christmas, there could be 12 for dinner, not including children. The adults were seated in the dining room, and the children were at their special table in the living room. To help in the kitchen, my mother hired a woman to assist in cooking, serving, and cleaning up.

At home, a typical evening started at 5:00 P.M. with a long cocktail hour. In my teenage years, I often served as a bartender so that my father could remain with his guests. In filling their requests, I harbored a secret that I later realized could have been dangerous. Two of the older women who came frequently were diabetic and had been ordered by their doctors to stop drinking. Since I did not know that they took advantage of my innocence and happily consumed one dry martini after another. They managed to hold their liquor, as the saying goes.

Christmas

Christmas on Matilija Road was a highlight of the year. Unlike many other Glendale residents, we did not spend a huge effort in decorating the outside of the house. My father thought it was a waste of time and money, as well as being too show-offish. We joined other curious people in traveling around the town in the evening to look at the outdoor displays that people, vying with one another, made with strings of Christmas lights, life-size cutouts of Santa Claus and angels, bushes adorned with fake snow and white lights, and Christmas music piped outside to speakers. Yes, we had a few strings of lights outside our house, but we saved our efforts for the living room, where a large tree was always the focus of attention.

We all got together and chose the tree at a local lot, but my father customarily insisted on decorating it himself. One year, he had the tree painted black and decorated it with only ornaments of silver and gold. Certainly, it was different as well as chic, but my mother, sister, and I preferred a more traditional look. Every year, he added more Christmas bulbs than before. Then, as I remember, he hung the tinsel, one strand at a time, so they would not bunch up on a branch but hang and sparkle individually. The rest of us were permitted to come into the living room at the end of his work and place an angel on top of the tree.

As in most families, Christmas meant the tree, of course, but more exciting was the giving of gifts. When you were little, you knew that the gifts came from Santa Claus, somehow miraculously sliding down the chimney and leaving them around the tree. But when you had grown up, you were just as excited even though you may have lost your belief in Santa's existence. On Christmas morning, my sister and I woke way too early for our parents' sake and could barely wait for them so that we could open the bulky stockings hung by the chimney with care, knowing that Santa Claus had been there. I opened my stocking to find the inevitable orange and apple. Then my mother would say, jokingly, "That's all you are getting this year because you have been a very bad boy." The next gifts were items you needed for daily life: socks, shirts, ties for the men, skirts, blouses, and perfume for the women. My mother always made new pajamas for her husband.

The special gifts—the ones you hoped for—came next. In our second year at the new house, I asked for a typewriter to show that I was serious about writing. They gave me a Remington formerly used in an office and in good shape. Next to the bicycle I had received several years before in our former house, this was my favorite gift of all time. My sister always knew what she was getting because it was her habit before Christmas to wait until the house was empty and then systematically open all the gifts tagged for her, unwrap the boxes, examine the contents, and then carefully wrap them as they were before. Then, of course, she feigned surprise when she opened them on Christmas morning, fooling nobody.

On one Christmas morning, my father did not give a present to our mother, and although she was happy with the few things she received from my sister and me, her husband appeared to have neglected her. He then tossed a ball of wadded wrapping paper at her. Thinking it was trash, she tossed it into the fireplace. My father leaped up, grabbed the ball of paper, and told her to open it. Inside was the diamond ring that she had been coveting. He got a big hug and kiss.

Ordinarily, he did not play practical jokes like that, so this stunt became a legend in our family.

After the ritual around the tree, we thanked each other for our gifts and had a grand breakfast. The rest of the day was devoted to making and receiving phone calls of goodwill. In the evening, our family's custom was to have Christmas dinner at home with a large group of friends and relatives. Thus, there was more fun and more gifts.

My Parents at Home

My mother was eight years younger than my father, and they made a handsome couple, whether greeting guests or going out to a dance or dinner. My mother was a charming and attractive woman with her dark hair, high cheekbones, and appearance in fine-looking clothes, many of which she made herself, as was common for women in those days. Throughout her life, she maintained her figure and habit of dressing very well. My father, who became bald at 33, was equally good-looking. His tailor ensured that he cut a fine figure in handsome suits, shirts, ties, and shoes. He never discarded his suits, timeless in style and quality, and gave some of them to me when I went off to college, which made me one of the best-dressed men on campus.

Mon and Dad were members of the Armenian Allied Arts Association, a cultural and social organization that held art exhibitions, lectures, and monthly dances. They were both fond of the arts and, in their own artistic efforts, produced everything from mosaic panels (father) to plates made from enamel fused to copper (mother). They took great pleasure in seeing that our gardens were carefully planted and maintained, and although neither one of them played a musical instrument, they attended concerts and were excellent dancers.

Overall, I would say that in addition to being a very happily married couple, they were caring but strict parents. They set a good example for proper manners and were quick to correct us when necessary. Such manners, as standing when an adult entered the room, seem old-fashioned now. They also set a very high standard for loving and marrying, scorning divorce when it happened among friends or relatives. For them, a marriage was forever, and should that seem impossibly old-fashioned today, it set the perfect example for me. Edgar and I remained in a happy relationship for forty years until he died.

During these years, I worked regularly on weekends at odd jobs and the clothing store mentioned earlier, and in my spare time, I learned to drive. The California vehicle law at that time permitted an adolescent to get a learner's permit if he or she was 12 years old and able to reach the gas and brake pedals with their feet. That has since changed to a requirement of 16 years. I qualified and soon was borrowing one or the other of my parents' cars to go on dates. When I reached my senior year in high school, I'd saved enough money to buy my own car, a used Ford coupe in good condition. In college, I kept it until, again using savings, I sold it and bought my dream car, an Austin-Healey Sprite. I kept that car until 1967, and when I was ready to leave for the East Coast, I was told that New York City was no place for a sports car, so I bought a practical Volkswagen convertible to take its place. I kept it for two years and sold it. When I needed a car to drive to work at Pratt Institute in Brooklyn, I bought an Infiniti sedan.

The Barsam Family and the Movies

The movie industry, with five major studios and several minor ones, made Southern California a mecca for those who wanted to work in them, not just would-be actors but other artists and technicians of all kinds. The major studios were in Culver City, Burbank, and Hollywood. Glendale was close enough to all of them to make an ideal place to live. Glendale was especially attractive to those who worked at Warner Bros. and Walt Disney studios, both within a ten-minute drive.

Our family has a history and connection with the movie business. As I previously wrote, my mother's career as a movie actress began and ended with a tiny role in a Paramount Pictures production. She was on the screen for only twenty-three seconds. My father was much more fortunate in establishing a dry-cleaning service for the studio. He became a friend of Harry Carey, a movie actor who began his career in the first decade of the 20th century in films by D. W. Griffith and John Ford and went on to make more than one hundred movies in various genres between 1908 and 1948 and best known for his work in Westerns.

Carey lived on a vast ranch named San Francisquito, in the country North of Glendale. It was the production site of many

Hollywood movies, especially Westerns, and a showcase for the Native American people who appeared in those films and entertained the tourists who visited the site. A group of his friends, including my father and his brother Meran, formed a weekend group there for fellowship, carousing, and hunting. He told me wonderful stories about the place.

My father's niece Betty took the family's contact with the movie business a step further when she married William M. Graf, who started his career as an assistant to Harry Cohn, the head of Columbia Pictures, and then became an assistant director and producer for film mogul Sam Spiegel, and ended his career as the head of Columbia's London office which was responsible for all the studio's films made outside the United States. The Grafs, our closest relatives, were often guests for dinner. Bill entertained us with fascinating stories about his work, with Spiegel's Horizon Pictures, on such films as John Huston's The African Queen and David Lean's The Bridge on the River Kwai and Lawrence of Arabia. My father, who was entranced by these stories, was a longtime investor in the stock market, and it was the success of the Huston film that encouraged him to invest in Horizon Pictures in the late 1950s at Bill Graf's suggestion. It was probably the most lucrative investment of my father's life.

Between 1971 and 1983, Card Walker was the Chief Executive Officer of The Walt Disney Company, the only person to hold that power who was not a member of the Disney family. His family lived in Flintridge, North of Glendale, and although I don't know the story, he and his wife became friends with my father and mother. They were often seen together dining out. Impressed with the Disney company's diversification into entertainment other than movies, he invested in the company. Although the Disney company was ordinarily a very sound investment, the stock market took a major fall and caused a great loss for all concerned. I was then living in New York and wasn't aware of the situation until my father phoned to say he had just lost a fortune, adding, "Don't tell your mother."

Ordinarily, my father was a very shrewd investor, as he was with all financial matters, but he seldom, if ever, mentioned it to the family. He may have talked about it with my mother, I don't know, but when I was in college and interested in the movie business, he told me some highs and lows of his investing career. I questioned him about his secrecy, and he simply said he didn't want people to know about it because they would gossip about it. He was a humble man when it came to money, working very hard to make his success, and never boastful about it.

Before WW II, the San Fernando Valley, some 260 square miles large, was cultivated in some areas for fruit trees, but otherwise, it was desert. The further Northwest and Northeast one traveled, the more barren it was. At the top of the region, the Tujunga Canyon provided much of the water needed for the development of Southern California. The property was cheap because few people imagined that one day, with the later access to water, the whole area would soon be developed with housing for the thousands of men and women returning from military service. My father bought several large parcels of land in Pacoima and its outskirts and refused to sell it until development reached that area. Little towns like Chatsworth, Mission Hills, Pacoima, and San Fernando itself began to grow and flourish as new water sources transformed the desert. There was a running joke in Hollywood at that time that Bob Hope owned one-half of the San Fernando Valley, as did Lucille Ball, Bing Crosby, Clark Gable, and Bette Davis, who each owned another half. None of them owned that measure of property, but many members of the movie colony owned land there. As developments began, land prices soared, and Papa sold, a very wise and sound decision.

As for the movies, I did not know then that they would become a major part of my teaching and writing career. Through my high school and college years, and with helpful family connections, I visited several studios to watch movies being made. It all started when Anna Graf, Bill's sister and an assistant to Henry Blanke, a movie producer at Warner Bros, was able to arrange for me a visit to the set of A Star is Born, the version with Judy Garland. She, like many actors, insisted on working on a closed set, one restricted to only workers on the film; in other words, no visitors. Breaking that rule, Anna, who was friends with Garland, persuaded director George Cukor to let me watch a dance rehearsal with the condition that I sit out of sight and be quiet. That day, Garland was having a difficult time working with a large group of male dancers for one of the movie's major scenes. Suddenly, she spotted me, came down from the stage where she was working, and then, pointing a sharp finger at me, demanded of Cukor, "Who is that?" with a heavy emphasis on the word who. He explained that I was a member of Anna Graf's family, as well as a film student at

USC. Surprisingly, she relaxed and chatted with me, finally saying that I could remain if I stayed in the chair and didn't talk. I agreed.

It is a great leap backward in time to go from Judy Garland to Gloria Swanson, the most famous of all silent movie actresses. When I was in high school, I heard that Swanson came to Glendale to visit her mother every Thursday afternoon at her house on Kenneth Road. I encouraged a few school friends to join me in going to see a movie star in person. We rode our bikes to the house and waited. Soon, a classic chauffeur-driven Rolls-Royce, the mellow color of root beer, turned into the driveway and stopped. Her stately exit from the car was worthy of Norma Desmond, as she learned that three high school boys were waiting for her. Graciously, she talked to each of us individually, about ourselves, not herself. Many years later, I was involved in negotiations with Leni Riefenstahl, the controversial German film director, to write her biography, but we could not agree on terms. In the meantime, she, Swanson, and Francis Ford Coppola were invited to the first Telluride Film Festival in the Rockies to receive a Lifetime Achievement Award. Riefenstahl asked me to accompany her on the trip to Colorado. At a dinner honoring those three film greats, an unlikely combination of talents, I was seated next to Swanson, and when I mentioned that we'd met before, she remembered meeting a group of movie-loving kids in front of her mother's house in Glendale.

One of Bill Graf's close friends was Walter Strohm, an MGM executive who started out at the studio in his teens and worked his way up to become a production manager. There wasn't anything going on at MGM that Walter didn't know. When I was writing my master's thesis on F. Scott Fitzgerald's period as a scriptwriter in Hollywood, including his unhappy stint at MGM, Walter got me access to MGM's archives, which enabled me to read and use valuable information that had not previously been published. Strohm also knew Gary Meadows, my best friend at USC, and he took both of us to MGM previews.

Walter and his good friend, director George Cukor, were closeted gay men. The many gay stars hid behind hollow marriages designed to make them seem otherwise. I knew just how private (and public) Hollywood personalities could be, so I was delighted when Cukor invited Gary and me to one of his famous parties. He also invited members of the USC football and swimming teams to entertain us with their zany behavior in the swimming pool. Afterwords they joined us for lunch.

In another part of the garden was the guesthouse that Spencer Tracy and Katherine Hepburn used for their long-term affair. These top stars were also longtime friends of Walter Strohm, which gave me the opportunity to meet Hepburn. It happened this way. In 1967, after I had moved to New York, Hepburn was making a rare Broadway appearance in the musical "Coco," based on the life of Coco Chanel. Although Hepburn started her career in the New York theater, this was her only appearance in a musical. Strohm had come to New York to see the show and took me and Gary along as his guests. Afterward, we went backstage to greet Hepburn. When she heard Strohm's name, she bounded out of her dressing room in a hallway and cried out for all to hear: "Why, Walter Strohm, you old son-of-a-bitch!" After they talked, Hepburn, with the charm you would expect from such a grand lady, greeted Gary and me before disappearing into her dressing room.

Chapter Seven:
High School

1952-1954

Herbert Hoover High School, located on Glenwood Road across from Toll Junior High, was named in 1929 for the 31st President of the United States. The impressive main building anchors a distinctive campus. The city's other high school, on the Eastern side of town, opened in 1901 and was simply named Glendale High School. My expectation was that high school would expand my knowledge with a new and higher level of teaching, classroom discussions, tests, and grading. At the same time, I hoped that I would have at Hoover a positive social experience with new friends and activities, but that was not more important than education. Looking back, all three years there were a pleasurable experience, both academically and socially. It was also time to start thinking about colleges and to apply to those that attracted me. We'll start there because it takes three years to complete the process.

Applying For College

Academically, I earned satisfactory grades at Toll but did much better at Hoover, maintaining a B+ average throughout. Even though it was an academic high school (Glendale did not have special. high schools that prepared students for various trades), less than half of my graduating class went on to college. Hoover had advanced placement

(AP) courses that are specifically taught for those preparing for college. In my day, though, the process for choosing students for AP courses was a secret effort by teachers and academic counselors who, if they deemed you eligible, chose courses for you. For the teachers' pets—sons and daughters of physicians, attorneys, and business executives—who had no problem with this process, it was assumed that they should have these classes. To me, it seemed to be rank favoritism, as insidious as the so-called legacy admission was at some of the best colleges. Either you were chosen for one of these special classes, or you were overlooked, and while there was an appeals process, it did not work. I was not chosen for any AP classes—my family was not in the elite group—but that did not influence my plans for going to college.

In my junior year of high school, I reaffirmed my decision to go to college. For those with that ambition, it was necessary to meet with the school's counseling staff to review their grades and other qualifications to determine eligibility. My counselor was Miss Gertrude Block (not her real name), a bookkeeping and typing instructor. Those seem like unusual qualifications for advising students on academic issues as serious as choosing a college. My choices for college were Stanford, UCLA, and USC, and my grades were above average and suitable for any of these schools, my record of extra-curricular activities was strong, and I had passed the SAT exam. Nevertheless, without discussing any of these qualifications, the stern, clueless Miss Block plunged right in to say—with her own peculiar logic—that since neither of my parents had attended college,

I should forget my aspirations and think instead of a trade school. "What trade school?" I queried, to which she replied, "Plumbing or carpentry." I thought she was making a joke, but she was serious. Even now, some seventy years on, this moment seems unbelievable. I told her that I would discuss that with my parents, and the next day, my father found himself in her office.

While I was not present at their meeting, he told her that he did not raise his son to be a plumber or a carpenter and saw no reason why I should not submit my applications. He added that both he and my mother strongly encouraged Miss Block to change her mind and recommend me. The fact that neither had a college education was not an acceptable issue. He was a man to speak the truth, not make threats. In so doing, he had exposed a genuine flaw in the school's counseling services. Some months later, when I received acceptance letters from the three colleges and showed them to Miss Block, she seemed a little baffled but nonetheless managed to congratulate me. I despair now to think how many other qualified students she steered away from higher education.

Memorable High School Teachers

My high school teachers were more honest than Miss Block in recommending and preparing me for college. For example, my senior year history teacher, Mrs. Alice MacDonald, a Ph.D. from the University of Chicago, not only recommended useful books to me but also taught me how to prepare and write a full-dress research paper. After a great deal of research and note-taking, I submitted a 20-page typed essay, with footnotes, on the origins of American jazz music. She gave me an A grade.

Other memorable teachers included Mildred Pierce (no connection to the great movie of that name), who taught me French with a stern emphasis on proper pronunciation; Gordon Footman, an English teacher with a wicked sense of humor; Marian Grey, with whom I worked backstage on student productions and learned a lot about the theater; and the feisty Ruppert Matthews, who also taught English and was the faculty advisor to the Purple Press the bi-weekly student newspaper (purple and White were the school colors). I took his journalism course in my junior year and was elected by the other students to head the newspaper's staff in my senior year, a position I found more responsible, interesting, and rewarding than anything else in my high school years. I also served as an editor of the senior yearbook titled simply Scroll.

Then there was the geometry teacher Estelle Spry, in whose mathematics class I could never get better than a D or F no matter how hard I worked. I had always been weak in math and science, but geometry was necessary for college admission, and I had to learn it. So, during my first year, on her own and refusing compensation, she spent several Saturdays each week during the summer tutoring me in geometry until I could get a passing grade and not disgrace myself on the college entrance exams. She was memorable in other ways also because she was a wealthy woman who did not need to work. With her flaming red hair, Mrs. Spry stood out among faculty members—

she refused to teach anything but geometry and trigonometry—and I adored her, even though I am still uncomfortable with mathematics.

Some High School Memories

Most of my high school memories were good ones. I was part of the intellectually inclined group that was headed for college. In addition to being the editor-in-chief of the student newspaper, I was elected to several student committees. As for sports, I was big enough for baseball or football but didn't have any interest in trying to join the teams. Furthermore, I lacked the balance and coordination to participate in sports. Sports were everything to many boys. My passion was literature, and I devoted my free time to reading the great American novelists and playwrights, their books, and their biographies. I also liked the movies and sought out the theaters in Los Angeles that showed high-quality foreign films. I also visited art museums, trying to get as much of the local culture that existed at the time. My parents subscribed to The New Yorker, which taught me that Manhattan supported a vast world of culture and, as I used to say, somewhat pretentiously, I felt that I was born in the wrong town and was somehow destined to live in New York City.

My only bad memory was of being bullied by a hulking lout named John Ingram (not his real name), the son of a notorious Glendale police officer known for his rudeness and lack of judgment. Being somewhat younger than the other students, I was a natural target for bullying. Previously, I had never had any contact with Ingram nor done anything that might have angered or offended him.

Unfortunately, his hall locker was next to mine. One day, as I removed the brown paper bag containing the lunch my mother prepared for me, he grabbed it, threw it on the ground, and stomped on it until it was destroyed. He said nothing and just walked away, and there was no profit for me in responding. He was obviously a disturbed young man, a classic bully, and there was something symbolic about his behavior that further bothered me. Knowing the effort and love that my mother always put into my lunches (even the vegetarian ones), I imagined that he was stomping on her, not the bag. He did not know my mother, and I regard his act as a symbol of unexplained hatred or resentment or just plain cruelty or all these things. I did not want any trouble and did not report it to the principal's office or even tell my friends, but I still remember that moment when I think of high school.

Activities Outside of School

When at Hoover, I became interested in politics and helped to organize "We Like Ike," an Eisenhower-for-President movement for teenagers, a rather futile effort because we were too young to vote. My parents were Democrats, and I eventually became a dedicated Democrat for the rest of my years. But during the hot summers of 1952 and 1953, I was invited by two friends to join them in an effort I call inspired lunacy, known only to the three of us. I refer to the founding of the Institute of Zbojniewicism (pronounced baz-nee-wi-cisim). What this imaginary institution stood for is beyond remembering, but not unusual considering the many religious, philosophical, or health cults in Southern California, some legitimate, many phonies. Zbojniewicism had no agenda except to provide us with fun. We each adopted zany names, had stationery printed with those names, and corresponded endlessly on those hot summer days, sending our letters by special delivery, which in those days cost only a quarter. As I was writing this, I found some of these communications in my files and remembered the nuttiness of it all. Clearly, it was a very private activity, which stopped before our senior year of high school, when preparing for college became more important than nonsense.

I became friends with Walt Jenkins (not his real name), who came from a prosperous and active social family. To me, he was a fascinating friend, five years younger than me, and the rebel in his family. Although he did well in high school, he frustrated his parents' expectations by riding a motorcycle, working in a local gas station, and not showing any interest in going to college. We then had little in common, but we nonetheless got along very well. One evening, while listening to some Bach recordings with his sister at their house, he came in and listened with us and later said he wanted to know more about the composer. And I wanted to know more about him as I had developed a slight crush on him. I introduced Walt not only to Bach but also to books by Tolstoy, of whom he was especially fond. He was soon borrowing other books from my library. After we became closer friends, he organized a camping trip for the two of us to Yosemite National Park.

After loading the car with camping gear, we headed out, taking turns in driving. We spent a week in Yosemite, camped next to a stream, cooked our dinners on an outside fire, drank perhaps too much wine, and slept side by side in the tent. Later, when I was in college, I kept track of Bill, and after he graduated from Hoover, I was surprised to hear that he did not want to go to college. I kept encouraging him, saying he was too smart to ignore the experience and what it would mean for his future. He was accepted at UCLA, majored in economics, and later got a job as an accountant in the US Forest Service (USFS) office at Yosemite. His first wife did not like living in the comparative wilderness of Yosemite, and they eventually divorced. He married again, but the second wife died young from cancer. He married for the third time, and they moved to New Jersey, where he moved up to being an executive in the USFS. He continued his love of music, and his wife introduced him to the Metropolitan Opera, where they became regular patrons. I heard from him several times, but we never seemed to get together. When his third wife died, he phoned to tell me that he listened to Bach for days on end while grieving and that he was forever grateful to me for introducing him to his music.

Social Life

In high school, many of us thought of sex as an uncertain and unfamiliar activity, although there were other students who were doing whatever with whomever. I did not think about being gay, although I had a silent crush on several handsome football players, two of whom turned out to be gay a few years later. But aside from my earlier liaison with the theater director, I did not have any sexual contact with other males. Instead, I dated girls and went steady with

Linda Lawson (not her real name). We decided to both apply to attend USC.

We liked dancing, which in those days meant ballroom dancing of various kinds, especially the fox trot and the waltz. One learned to do these well at Jane Denham's Cotillion, a series of classes for young people our age. Those young people came from the elite families of Glendale. Participation was by invitation only, and when I received the acceptance letter from Miss Denham, I was happy to be in that social crowd. At the monthly dances, boys were required to wear suits and ties, girls wore long formal dresses, and at the final dance of the season, boys wore tuxedos. To make sure we behaved like young ladies and gentlemen, parents were invited to chaperone these dances. I danced with my steady girlfriend, who was also a member and had a nice choice of other dancing partners. In old-fashioned style, each young woman had a little book in which she listed the boys who had asked her to dance that night. My good friend Marilyn Neeley, who went on to become an internationally known concert pianist, was often my partner. But Marilyn simply didn't like dancing, and thus, we hid behind the drapes in the ballroom, so we didn't have to participate. We got away with this prank several times and were lucky not to have been discovered. Her mother disapproved of our friendship, such that when we studied together at the Neeley's house, she sat down with a book and never left the room. I managed to keep in touch with Marilyn, and after I moved to New York, she wrote to tell me she was giving a piano recital at Lincoln Center and invited me to attend the concert and a small dinner afterward. When I arrived at the dining room, I approached Mrs. Neeley to greet her, and all she said was, "What are you doing here?" All I could say in response was that Marilyn had invited me. By then, Marilyn had married and had a son. I was no longer a threat, but the mother thought otherwise.

There was another Marilyn in my life, Marilyn Monroe, on whom I had an understandable crush. This was confirmed by the full-length nude photograph pinned to the back of my closet door. When my mother saw it, she seemed rather pleased and said that this made me seem like other boys. As you will find later in the book, I once got very close to the real Marilyn Monroe.

By then, we all had driver's licenses, which gave us the freedom to go almost anywhere we liked, including trips to the beach, to the mountains for camping trips, movies in Hollywood, and various excursions to interesting spots in Southern California. It would be years before Los Angeles developed a cultural life equal to that of, say, San Francisco, but nevertheless, there was a developing world of theater, opera, classical music, and art museums. It was fun to drive through the many agricultural areas around L.A. that still had fresh, clean air, open land, unpaved roads, small farms, and fruit and avocado ranches. While it was memorably beautiful then, it soon disappeared with the growth of the post-war population, new industries, huge tracts of new houses, freeways, and the inevitable smog, enough to turn the blue skies brown.

With high school almost finished, college would be the next major period in my life. But in the 1950s, a college education did not represent the automatic key to success that it does for some people today. Only a small group of my college class chose to go to college. The others married their high school sweethearts, had children, and followed in their father's business or profession. Very few remained single. Whatever path they followed, they remained in Southern California, where, according to the report issued at the 60th class reunion, 66% of the graduates still lived in Glendale or nearby.

Every ten years, the Hoover alumni organize a dinner-dance reunion at the Oakmont Country Club. Did I attend them? One year, they asked me to attend and give a brief speech about my life in Manhattan. Although I thought about it, I declined because showing up with one of my gay partners didn't seem appropriate for the occasion. Today, of course, that wouldn't be an issue. I've read that most high school graduates avoid these gatherings. It's easy to see why, for they struggle with the changes they would see in former friends, like the handsome football quarterback who is now overweight and bald after fifty years, and the Prom Queen, who has lost her looks and charm.

Bad Memories

The worst memory comes not when I was still in high school but (briefly jumping forward in time) in my first year at USC. I missed my former Hoover classmates, particularly Jerry Davis, with whom I kept in contact. He was a moody fellow but fun to be with and had not entered college, although he was a brilliant student. When I received a phone call from his mother, I was shocked to hear that he had hanged himself in the garage. His reason was unknown to me, and my grief was deep. The family wanted a private funeral and asked me to attend, saying that I was his only friend. Hearing that made me feel even worse and wondering if there was anything I could have done to help him. But it was not the only suicide that upset my life.

Suzanne Welch, a neighbor, classmate, and as involved in extra-curricular activities as anyone could be, was also one of the great beauties at Hoover High. After graduation, she was determined to go to New York and become a clothes designer. Instead, she became a model. On my summer trip to New York in 1964, she was the first person I visited after getting off the plane. She lived in Greenwich Village, and I spent my first night sleeping on her floor. Time passed, and things must have changed for her, for she returned not to Glendale but to her family's ranch near Reno, Nevada. Some years later, when I was in graduate school, she invited me to visit her there. On the drive to Nevada, I saw not only Las Vegas and Lake Tahoe but also the notable Basque sheepherders with whom we shared one of their legendary meals.

Suzanne and I went to see Liberace, the famous pianist-comedian, was performing at a Reno casino. Opening the show for him was a relatively unknown young singer who had just had success in a Broadway show and was making a tour to promote her first record album. Her name was Barbra. We got to hear Liberace play while Streisand sang. After a few more days enjoying the ranch, I returned to Los Angeles. Some weeks later, I was shocked for the second time by a phone call from Suzanne's father, who informed me that she had committed suicide, also by hanging. I mourned Jerry and Suzanne, who were among the best and the brightest, as well as among the most promising of my friends. They ended their lives before giving life a chance.

Looking back, I understand that high school graduation marked a major turning point in my life. For twelve years, I was educated and guided by the Glendale school system. But it was another stronghold of conformity Excepting certain unique administrators and teachers, it was a system that discouraged individuality and independence. There was something militaristic in the insistence that we toe the line and stand up straight, and it's no surprise that the ROTC was a key extra-curricular activity for male students at Hoover High. In addition, as I have written, the high school maintained a dishonest caste system with certain influential teachers favoring students who may not have been their best and brightest but whose families were wealthy or community leaders. This made me angry but not jealous. What gain could this bring those misguided counselors? What loss was suffered by those students that they ignored or misled? Discipline was what they wanted us to learn, not the assets of loyalty, integrity, honor, respect, and kindness, qualities I was lucky enough to learn from my parents.

At this point in my life, the best that I can say about myself is that I was competent academically, not smart enough to be invited to join the Honor Society or make the valedictory address at graduation, but nonetheless well-prepared at sixteen to face the first of the many challenges I would encounter in the coming years. And I was about to leave home, aside from summer camp, and live at the college.

Chapter Eight:
College Life

1955-1959

For a young person, choosing a college is one of life's most important decisions in one's life. It will be a factor in one's intellectual, psychological, and social growth and well-being, to name just a few. Whether one chooses a public or a private college, the principal considerations remain much the same: the institution's mission and reputation, the requirements of the academic program in which one plans to major, and the cost of tuition and room and board. My high school friends chose colleges relatively close to home, whether it was Oregon, Arizona, Colorado, or California. Going to a college in the eastern part of the country meant not only leaving home for long periods of time but also involved of traveling long distances, with rail, bus, or car the only reasonable possibilities until jet airplanes began flights in 1959.

Because I would be entering college at the age of sixteen, as contrasted to most freshmen who are eighteen, I applied to three California colleges. Stanford University in Palo Alto is a private institution with an excellent academic reputation, especially in preparing graduates for careers in engineering, medicine, science, law, and computer science. My next choice was the University of California at Los Angeles (UCLA), famous for its high academic expectations within the public university world. It occupies an impressive campus in Westwood, bordering Beverly Hills. The University of Southern California (USC), which was my preferred choice, is a private institution situated on a campus near downtown Los Angeles. Like UCLA, it offers a full range of academic programs, including the professional schools of law, business, engineering, and architecture. All three colleges had fraternities, competitive football teams, and good reputations. I would have been happy if any one of those selected me.

I was overwhelmed that all three accepted me, and I chose USC. This meant that I could have a first-rate education while living near my parents. Eventually, the total time I spent in college was divided into two parts: my undergraduate years, during which I earned a B.S. in Business, and my graduate school years, where I earned an M.A. and Ph.D. in English Literature. I also did an independent study of film history and production at USC's School of Cinema.

Before beginning college, however, I aspired, like my father, to be an architect. While still in high school, I spent my free time studying and photographing the many buildings designed by Frank Lloyd Wright (FLW) in the Los Angeles area. From this informal study, I reached the conclusion that the art of architecture was either engineering or poetry, sometimes both. Like many others, I consider Wright to be the greatest poet of twentieth-century architecture. However, I was to learn that studying architecture would prove to be the wrong road to take in my first year in college.

Enrolling in the USC School of Architecture program required a year of physics as a prerequisite, which was a major challenge for me because, in high school, I rejected physics in favor of chemistry and avoided mathematics any higher than geometry. So, with little enthusiasm, I registered for a two-semester course on physics. At the end of the first semester, I took a short trip to bolster my enthusiasm and knowledge. During the winter break, I joined a group of like-minded students from other colleges to attend a two-week session for potential apprentices at FLW's Taliesin compound in Scottsdale, Arizona. We were assigned individual tents and spent our days in the master's workroom, where his staff—all architects trained by him—were transforming his beautifully detailed drawings into blueprints ready for construction. At the end of the day, we all ate together and, following dinner, were treated to a movie, a concert, a poetry reading, or a talk from the master himself. On the first night, Mr. Wright asked me to sit on the floor beside him. I couldn't imagine why he would choose the youngest person in the room, except that he may have become interested when earlier I had shown him the album of my photos of his buildings. While sitting on the floor and watching a Japanese movie, I felt FLW stroking my head of curly hair. I didn't know how to interpret that intimacy, which became his habit. His wife Olgivanna sat close to him and didn't seem to mind the attention he paid to me, which I decided was all in friendship. Nevertheless, for the next two weeks, I was repeatedly teased for being "Frank's boy."

When I returned to USC, I began the second semester of physics. While I believed that I might find some kind of beauty in learning physics, I believed even more that architecture was poetry, not engineering. Maybe that was what FLW reinforced in my brain as he tousled my curls. Yet, the hard truth is that I failed both semesters of physics. The Dean of Architecture politely suggested that I choose another major. Ironically, my father had no time or money for education. Yet, he studied all he could find about architectural design, and as you will see later, he was proud of a design he made plan for the construction of a new house. But I was not proud of anything, for, at the end of my freshman year, I had made a poor academic performance and wasted my father's money.

Planning to be an architect was not the only mistake I made in my first year in college; the other was joining a fraternity. After a rush week, I was tapped for the pledge class of Phi Kappa Tau. In all fraternities, if you could hold your liquor, you were accepted into the group; if you couldn't, you could be ignored. Some of the older members, who were Korean War veterans, did well academically, but drinking was another major activity. The legal age for drinking in California was twenty-one, and I turned seventeen in my freshman year. I managed to fit in but wasn't taught how to drink, when to drink, or how much to consume. When I think about it, I realize that my father should have done that. The fraternity's social calendar included various weekly get-togethers, as well as two major dinner-dance parties at a country club, one each semester. Because I had some suggestions for improving these activities, I was chosen to be the fraternity's social secretary, in charge of planning these events.

It was time to choose my new academic major, and because I had a secret desire to be in the movie industry, I imagined myself as a producer like Bill Graf, my first cousin. His friend Walter Strohm, who was one of MGM's production managers, arranged for me to have a special visit to the MGM lot, the largest movie-making operation in the world. I thought this might mean an encouragement to work there. In fact, they tried to discourage my enthusiasm for being a producer by saying, "You don't have the balls for what it takes to work in this industry." As I became more and more familiar with the business end of the industry, in which movies were judged by box office receipts rather than their worth as works of art, I knew they were correct. I didn't have the cut-throat shrewdness that is plainly necessary to be a success in the motion picture industry.

Facing reality, I agreed with my academic counselor that the marketing and advertising majors in the School of Commerce might suit my interests. Advertising is a highly public and competitive world, like the movies, but I believed I had the balls for it. I was attracted by how ideas and products were designed and sold. The level of student creativity in the advertising and marketing classes was impressive, and I received outstanding grades for the work required. At the same time, I took almost enough courses in English Literature to earn the credits for a degree in that field, but did not have the time to complete the work. Later, I received a Ph.D. in English Lit.

Sex on Campus

One of the reasons that I chose marketing and advertising was that Linda Lawson, my high school girlfriend, was already studying those subjects. She pledged to a top sorority and was soon wearing my fraternity pin, the sure sign in the college of a committed relationship. Finding a time and place for sex was difficult for us. In addition, I had begun having sexual encounters with men and knew that this would likely be my future preference. Because I had respect and love for Linda, I made the painful choice to break our relationship. She did not take the news sympathetically and soon was seen around campus on the arm of a USC star athlete.

I thought I had given up women for good when a new friend, Don Beckwith—a cinema major, closeted gay man, and my unfulfilled crush—introduced me to Susan, an art major. They knew each other from La Jolla, where they came from wealthy families. Our relationship was casual, but I idealized her so much—I cannot remember why—that I was too shy to go any further than a goodnight kiss. One weekend, she left for a few days to attend a party her parents were giving. She invited me, only to discover when I got to her family's impressive house in La Jolla that the party was to announce her engagement to a long-time beau. She had been stringing me along, too cool to be touched but warm enough to enjoy my company without saying a word about the other man. Yet the future groom welcomed me to the party, saying that she'd told him things about me. Whatever, I was strong enough to survive the disappointment.

This experience increased my sensitivity to the issues of class and wealth, so when I met Joyce Peyton, a fellow student with whom I soon fell in love, I moved slowly. Joyce was a Black woman, born in England, schooled in France, and daughter of a notable American surgeon. She was a striking and beautiful figure on campus. Many men had tried to date her, but she only said yes to me. She was not bothered that I had previously had sex with men, and we began a limited sexual relationship. Joyce had a medical condition that slightly limited the use of her right leg, so she walked with a cane. This condition also limited her ability in bed. On campus, we were part of a creative group that shared a love of writing, so we established a student literary magazine we named Profiles. Joyce and I were the co-editors; a student committee chose the poems and short stories we published. The college gave us an office, a modest budget, and free access to its printing facilities. The story of my relationship with her will continue later.

During this time, I took a part-time job as an assistant in the office of the Dean of Liberal Arts and Sciences. This required me to be in his office for two hours on four afternoons a week; the pay was good, and I quickly got into the routine of a typical office: opening and sorting a large amount of mail, answering the phone if his secretary was busy with another caller, photocopying materials (the Xerox machine had not yet been invented), and, of course, making coffee. The Ddean took an interest in my studies and even offered to read one of my papers. And I learned to concentrate first on my education and put my social life second. My grades improved, and I felt that I was growing up, whatever that meant.

Fraternity in Trouble

In my third year in college, it came as a surprise, indeed a shock, to be elected President of my fraternity despite my protest. I quit my part-time job in the Dean's office and set out to do my best as the leader of the fraternity. In fact, it turned out to be a good experience that taught me to use my organizational abilities and reputation for getting things done on time, as well as how to work with fraternity brothers of different ages, backgrounds, interests, and accomplishments. As president, I sat at the head of the dinner table, got a private bedroom at the front of the main house, and made myself available for the other members and their problems. Fortunately, I was not responsible for the house's finances. They were handled by a part-time professional manager and former frat brother, who reported to me and handled all the business matters, including the budget, purchasing, and building repairs. He was also responsible for Mrs. Davis's kitchen, but not the cooking, which was quite good. I am proud that I helped to measurably improve the quality of life at that frat house.

Looking back, as I write, I know that beginning my senior year was the lowest point in my college education. All along fraternity row, the school year started with the rushing, choosing, and hazing of pledges. In a few houses, the hazing activities endangered the lives of these young men. During rush week, I was confronted with a very unusual situation. Dick Swanson, with whom I initially pledged Phi Kappa Tau three years before, stunned us all by announcing that he was quitting our fraternity and pledging to Kappa Sigma. He believed the other house had a social life more to his style. While I pleaded with him not to put his social life above his education, there was no stopping him.

What happened next was a tragedy that stunned the entire USC community. Kappa Sigma put its pledges through a hazing ordeal requiring them to swallow whole a large piece of beef liver without chewing it. His fellow pledges succeeded in the challenge, but Dick fought for breath, choking as he tried to swallow it on both the first and second efforts, and finally collapsed. The fire department responded, and when their resuscitator squad couldn't help him, they took him to a hospital, where, within two hours, he died at the age of twenty-one. The USC administration not only suspended Kappa Sigma from the campus but also put all members on probation and later banished it from the campus.

I regretted not being able to persuade Dick to stay with us, but I knew him to be intelligent, self-assured, and determined to do what he wanted, and I could not have done anything to change his mind. I grieved for him and felt that the right thing to do, in protest, was to resign immediately as a member and President of my fraternity. Several other frat brothers joined me in taking this position.

This incident, along with similar ones, plunged U.S. fraternities and sororities (known as the Greek community) into turmoil. Efforts were made to establish new rules for hazing, even to abolish it. In all of this, I was concerned about the community's use of the word "fraternity" when, in at least one USC frat house, it meant not brotherhood but a total disregard for human life. One of the brothers who agreed with me was Gary Yench, a sophomore member of the fraternity who had chosen me as his big brother. He quit also and proposed that we share an apartment, which I realized would be good for us both. Although we came from different backgrounds—he was raised in New York City—and had different academic interests—he was a pre-med student—we got along very well. Thus, we were lucky to find an available two-bedroom apartment on the top floor of a classic old coach house located behind one of the great mansions in the neighborhood adjacent to the campus. We had access to a large garden, and Gary convinced the owner to lower our rent in return for our mowing the lawn, watering the plants, and keeping the area tidy. That extra money helped us to pay the grocery bill.

Successful as this arrangement was, it ended in a few months when Gary moved in with his girlfriend. I also had to move but found an attractively furnished apartment in another old mansion, which I shared with an architecture student, another frat brother who also resigned in protest of Dick Swanson's death. We were both seniors finishing up our undergraduate education, and the apartment offered enough privacy for the two of us to work without interruption. After graduating, I planned to enroll in the USC graduate degree program in English. My grades were uniformly good, and while I didn't make Phi Beta Kappa, I was not ashamed of my achievements. Moreover, my faculty advisors in the English Department encouraged me to continue my studies. If I qualified with my work for the M.A., I would be eligible to enroll in the Ph.D. program. I took their advice, and in June 1959, I graduated at age twenty-one, and in the Fall enrolled in the USC Graduate School.

Chapter Nine: Graduate School

Jon Warner Enters My Life

On my first day as a graduate student in September 1959, handsome and soft-spoken Jon Warner entered my life as we entered a seminar on Chaucer's Canterbury Tales. After the class, Jon introduced himself and suggested that we have coffee and get acquainted, thus beginning an on-and-off relationship that lasted for the next 14 years. The following account covers that connection between 1959 and 1964. After that, I will return to 1959 and my story of graduate school.

Jon was born in Compton, a Los Angeles suburb now famous for being the birthplace of many famous hip-hop musical artists. His mother, who had worked as a clothes model, married Jon's father, had two sons, and then divorced to marry again to a man who owned a Chrysler car dealership. They were an upper-middle-class family living in a ranch-style house with a swimming pool. At the time, Jon lived at home and appeared to have a good relationship with his parents. He intended to get a master's degree in English at USC and was two years older than me.

At that first meeting over coffee, I was attracted by Jon's gentle manner. Some people have commented that I can be bold in meeting new friends, getting what I want, and not stopping until I do. But this time, it was Jon who was the aggressor. After seeing each other for just a month, we agreed to share the apartment that my architecture roommate had vacated. Looking back as I write, I know that this move was a big mistake. We barely knew one another, were both adjusting to being gay and settling in together was a major decision for two men in their twenties who had not had previous lovers.

I may have cared more for Jon than he did for me. He spent a lot of time away from me, going to bars with a German woman he knew from Compton. I soon realized that he was an alcoholic, unable to control his addiction. He drank until he was drunk, sometimes passing out. This did not seem to interfere with his studies, for he was a straight-A student. We slept together in the same bed, but our sexual relationship at first was awkward. For example, he would stop in the middle, light a cigarette, and act as if that was normal as he stopped our activity. He could also be rough and domineering, demanding sex the way he wanted it. His temperament was unpredictable, and alcoholism only stressed our insecure relationship. In living with this problem and thinking about it every day, I asked myself if I had some responsibility for it. "What did I do, or where did I go wrong?" I knew from reading about it and talking with others in the same position that it was not my fault. In a relationship such as ours, when one partner abuses alcohol, both suffer psychological, physical, and social distress.

Our apartment—on the ground floor of one of the grand, old Victorian-era houses in the USC neighborhood—had been beautifully furnished by the owner, Norman Hansen. Ordinarily, he didn't rent to students but made an exception for us because he was also gay. The apartment was spacious enough for large parties. In my role as the co-editor of Profiles, the student literary magazine, I arranged for a series of lectures from noted authors living in the L.A. area, including, among others, Dorothy Parker, Ray Bradbury, and Christopher Isherwood. After their lectures, we held a party at this apartment for some twenty guests, but while the first two authors declined invitations to attend, Mr. Isherwood came gladly. I was a fan of his work and found him to be affable and eager to discuss it with students. He was a great storyteller, a gay icon, and a great drinker, but by the evening's end, he was also drunk, so Jon and I wouldn't let him drive home alone. No matter, he said, and crawled under a table and went to sleep. The following morning, we had breakfast together, and he drove himself home.

Our landlord, a successful antique dealer, lived with his lover in a Mediterranean-style house in the Hollywood hills, which he said was previously the home of actor Errol Flynn. He told me that the best way to sell a house quickly in Hollywood was to say its former owner was a movie star. Norman and Jon bonded closely in a shared sense of humor and a love of drinking. Norman deliberately saw Jon without me, and I knew that Jon confided in him in a way he never did with me. Norman appeared to want Jon for himself. I was too mindful of doing well in college and didn't have much time for Norman's social world. They had much in common, but Jon remained with me.

Here, I must be honest about my drinking because I have been so direct about Jon's drinking habits, and I want you to know that, in my first two years at USC, liquor got me into trouble twice before I met him. The first occasion was at a fraternity party high in the Bel Air hills at the home of Nils Swenson, a frat brother (not his real name). When we learned that Nils's father had invited two neighbors to attend the party, we were astonished when Jascha Heifetz, then the most famous violinist in the world, and his wife Florence appeared. The couple mixed happily with the frat brothers and their dates. As the party got livelier, I was challenged to drink 140-proof Jamaican rum, a very strong drink guaranteed to make anyone drunk. Unfortunately for me, I drank too much, slipped and fell on the pool deck, and cut my head. Mrs. Heifetz came immediately to my rescue and took charge, successfully stopping the bleeding while someone called an ambulance. I was taken to the Beverly Hills emergency room and cleaned up and bandaged. The staff called my father, who drove over from Glendale and took me home. The ride was silent, with no lecturing, but I still had not learned my lesson about misusing liquor. But my Papa was so fascinated with hearing about the Heifetz couple that he forgave me.

 The second unfortunate experience was also an accident caused by drinking. This time, I was driving late at night on Olympic Boulevard, and being full of booze, I fell asleep at the wheel. The car jumped the curb and crashed into the wall of a gas station that had already closed for the night. My car suffered much more damage than the building, which was just scratched. The police arrived and first checked to see if I was hurt (I wasn't). They believed the story that I fell asleep and lost control of the car. Amazingly, they didn't give me a Breathalyzer test or a ticket for drinking while under the influence. I phoned the frat house and asked for someone to pick me up. Before leaving, though, I left a note for the station employees saying that I would be there the following morning to settle the matter and arrange for them to repair the damage to my car. I did not tell my parents about that incident.

During these first years together, and regardless of his drinking, Jon and I got along smoothly, meeting new friends and hosting parties. When we celebrated receiving our M. A. degrees that summer, I was twenty-two, and he was twenty-five. But as time passed, we were increasingly unable to make the relationship work, so in the middle of 1962, Jon and I split up. He remained in the apartment, and I moved home to Glendale. My sister had since married and moved to her own house, so my parents were happy to have my company. I was at the stage of the doctoral program where I could begin working on the dissertation.

Back at home, my typical day at the time consisted of driving to the USC campus, attending a seminar, doing library research, or discussing my progress with my faculty advisor. Following that, I would spend a few hours late in the afternoon at my part-time office job, after which I went home in time for dinner. Weary of this schedule, I took a part-time night job teaching English literature at Glendale Community College (GCC). Later, when I was making good progress on my dissertation, I had time to also teach a day class.

Within a year, the head of the English department asked me to become a full-time member of the GCC faculty, and I agreed because I wanted the teaching experience and could use the money. It left me with enough time and financial support to finish my dissertation. As for Jon, we occasionally talked on the phone, and when I mentioned this job to him, it was not long before he was also hired for a part-time job there. This inevitably brought us back together, and so we rented a modern hillside house in Glendale, just minutes away from the college. Living together again soon proved to be another mistake. Jon was a popular teacher and somehow managed to keep that away from the heavy drinking, nasty temperament, and mental and physical abuse it provoked in him. With Jon, I did not fight back or cannibalize his life as he did mine. Or to ask him to control his alcoholic intake. With all of this, it is no surprise that our relationship began to fall apart again. In addition, he and the English Department chairperson did not get along, and she asked him to resign. We gave up the house, I returned to living with my parents, and he moved back to an apartment in Hollywood near Norman's. We seldom talked, and the vicious cycle of our relationship continued.

I Move to New York City

In June 1967, I received my Ph.D. degree and moved to Manhattan. Since arriving there, the only contacts I had with Jon were a few phone calls. In 1968, he called to say he missed me and wanted to resume our relationship and get a job in New York. I don't know if he really needed me as a partner or just wanted to continue to torment me with his drinking. But I no longer loved him and tried to discourage him from coming to New York, but he came anyway. I had little time for him because, in addition to teaching, I was writing what was to be my first book and needed all the time I could get to work on it. He had received a degree in librarianship and hoped to find a job as a research librarian in a college library. Since I knew the chief librarian of the Hunter College library, I asked if he would interview Jon. Long story short, he was hired there and moved in with me on a trial basis. Again, expecting that this arrangement would not work out well, I was a fool to agree with it. Jon was drinking even more than usual, two or three vodkas in the morning before going to work. Ordinarily, he was not physically abusive, but one drunken night, when I finally told him I'd had enough and that he must move to his own apartment, he punched me in the face, breaking my nose. Repairing the damage was a costly and unpleasant experience for me, including the times I had to tell my new colleagues and friends that "my ex-boyfriend did it."

I gave him a week to get his own apartment and get out of my life. He did both those things. Next, he was fired by Hunter because of his drinking as had also got himself involved with a new friend, Bob, a successful interior designer. Bob bought a country house in Stone Ridge in upstate New York. Bob established a small retail housewares business there, hired a staff, and made Jon the manager. Although they stayed together for a few more years, Jon's drinking continued to be as much a problem for his new partner as it did for me. Bob, who was not a drinker, had little patience with Jon's overdoing it and finally broke up the relationship. At this point, Jon, who had no partner, was out of work and out of luck.

He moved back to California, where he not only revived his friendship with Norman, who rented him the same apartment we had first shared while in grad school. This repetition of his past behavior was predictable. He got a job at the UCLA library, where his heavy drinking before work again got him fired. He lived on money borrowed from his parents. Since I was living three thousand miles away and had lost touch with him, I was surprised to get a phone call from Norman Hansen on November 8, 1973, the day of my 35th birthday. He told me that Jon had killed himself in the apartment. I grieved the loss of this handsome, talented, intelligent man who could have lived a good life if he wanted to. However, he had another plan. If he was going to suffer, so should everyone around him. As Arthur Miller wrote in After the Fall, "A suicide kills two people . . . that's what it's for!"

We Return to 1959

We now return to when this chapter started in September 1959 in Los Angeles, and I began the M.A. program in English Literature. It was a challenging academic experience for me. After all the usual seminars, we were required to write an original thesis. Mine was on the unpublished film scripts that F. Scott Fitzgerald had written in Hollywood in the mid-1930s. At that point in his career, he was considered a has-been; his wife Zelda was in a mental hospital, and he was struggling with alcoholism. These circumstances forced him, for financial reasons, to accept unfamiliar but necessary work as a screenwriter at M-G-M. This job did not go well for him, for he openly viewed it with contempt, and after his work on several important movies, much of which was not used, the studio let him go in 1939. He died the following year of a heart attack, long before his masterpiece, The Great Gatsby (1925), was re-discovered, bringing him recognition as one of the greatest American novelists.

Hollywood screenplays were an unusual subject for a graduate thesis, yet my faculty advisor approved my plan for its originality. Research is a major component in any graduate thesis, and this offered me a good opportunity to do research in M-G-M's archives as well as conduct interviews with studio employees who had worked with Fitzgerald. My father offered to continue paying my tuition, but grateful for his support in the past four years, I insisted on paying half of it. To help me in this, I worked part-time as an advertising copywriter with Jay Chiat & Associates, at the time, the most creative and successful ad agency in Los Angeles. At first, I wrote ads for small accounts, using humor as my chief asset. My work satisfied Chiat, who offered me a full-time job on larger projects. I reminded him that after I earned my degree, I intended to move to New York City and become a college teacher. He scorned that decision but kept me on the payroll, and after one of my ads won an award for creativity, he gave me a raise. Almost a year before I finished my degree requirements, Chiat moved the firm to New York. As a result, I was out of a job. While I could have moved with the staff to New York and had a career in advertising, I knew that my place was in the academic world. A few years later, Chiat merged and became TBWA\Chiat\Day, making it the largest advertising agency in the world. All things being equal—which of course, they're not—I think I made the right decision to stay with my original career plans.

Having quit the job in the ad agency, I still needed an income to help with paying tuition, and I interviewed for a job with Duncan Scott & Company, a firm that sold advertising space in publications concerned with architecture and interior design. In our first interview, Peter Schulz, a 6' 3" Welshman and the manager of the firm, explained that my job was to overhaul the office's out-of-date filing system, which contained information essential to the work of the firm's sales force. I was unfamiliar with what he wanted, but I believed I could do it. I did research on the subject and consulted with Peter's sales force to learn what they needed, as well as with companies that supplied the units for such a system. Finally, I proposed a plan to Schulz. This may not seem much of a challenge, but it was an original undertaking, something that would have been easy to do with today's computers. He was pleased with the plan, and so we set about putting it into effect. He also supported my academic aspirations and my desire to work late at night when the office was closed. Sometimes I worked into the early morning hours but eventually got the job done. With the office closed, I could have unfettered access to all the files and information necessary to do my job without interrupting the employees. After the necessary equipment was installed and I had given an orientation session to the staff, I had little to do, but Pete kept me on the payroll.

In June 1961, I received the M.A. degree in English Literature and looked forward to a summer with a complete change of activity and scenery. So, Gary Meadows and I embarked on a three-month driving trip to Mexico, in which I did the driving. We carefully planned our routes and destinations and managed to visit many states, cities, and archeological sites, including Mexico City, Taxco, Monterrey, Guadalajara, Oaxaca, Acapulco, and Tulum, to name a few. We visited towns in the highest mountains, like Puebla and Cuernavaca. A highlight of the trip, though, was the Yucatán, a peninsula on the Gulf of Mexico, which is known not only for its fine beaches in Cancun but, most significantly, for its great number of surviving pre-Columbian Mayan buildings and archeological sites. It was a far cry from the tourist mecca it is today. We made a base in Merida, the Spanish Colonial city that became the capital of Yucata?. In addition to its sleepy charm, it had a Roman amphitheater, plazas, museums, and cathedrals. From there, we fanned out to visit the archeological treasures, beginning with El Castillo Chichen-Itzá, an overpowering pyramid that is one of the Seven Wonders of the World. We climbed the long, steep staircase to the top, where we found a large iguana lizard basking in the sun. One day, we crossed the border to Guatemala to visit Tikal, located in a rainforest, and the great mountain city of Chichicastenango, the home of a large community of indigenous Mayan people. It was a truly great trip.

When we stopped in Veracruz, a busy port, I carelessly bought from a street vendor a dish of cooked shrimp, and the next day, I was very sick. Indeed, I went to the hospital, where they diagnosed that

I'd swallowed some badly spoiled food. They checked me in for a stay that lasted two weeks. During this period, I couldn't keep any food down, causing me to lose some forty pounds. Gary stayed in a hotel and visited me daily, and after I was released, we resumed our trip, intent on taking the fastest and most direct route to return to California. We stopped in Puerta Vallarta for a few days to enjoy the sunshine and the beach, then drove on through Baja California to Tijuana and entered the U.S. at San Diego, California. At the first restaurant we saw, we ate the biggest salad they could make, for we had gone without fresh and safe greens for most of the trip.

The Years Spent Earning A Ph.D.

In September 1961, back at USC, I started the Ph.D. program in English Literature, but Gary surprised me with a different plan. Although he had received a U.S. government scholarship that would fully support him while earning a doctoral degree, he turned it down and moved to New York City to take a job in publishing. He encouraged me to go with him, but I was determined to finish my degree first.

In early 1962, I passed the interview and entrance exams and was officially on my way to completing the doctoral program. It took almost six years and required attendance and participation in two seminars each semester for two years, then annual reviews of progress, a daunting set of final qualifying exams consisting of written answers to questions on four different areas of literature. The final step was to write a dissertation, essentially a book-length essay that should meet professional standards of research and make an original contribution to its field of study. It's not over yet. Professor Mary Mahl, my faculty advisor, regarded my manuscript as acceptable. After that, I made an oral defense of the work before a faculty committee, which approved it. Satisfying all these requirements made me eligible for the degree.

Joyce Peyton and Me

Through all these years, I maintained a close friendship with the wonderful Joyce Peyton, whom I hope you have not forgotten. We discussed marrying, realizing the difficult issues involved, but wanted the support of both our families. So, we first went to our fathers. These two men were very different in every way, but they shared a love for their children. Dr. Peyton was a renowned physician, born in the U. S. and trained in France, where it was easier in the 1920s for a Black man to study medicine and pay for his tuition with the money earned playing jazz piano in Paris nightclubs. He later moved to London, where, known for medical expertise in his field, he was sought out by Winston Churchill, whom he treated for several years. When Joyce was born, the former British Prime Minister was asked, as her godfather, to hold the child at her christening in Westminster Abbey.

My father's background was not as distinguished but equally interesting. My father told Dr. Peyton the story of his coming to America and the obstacles he had faced, and Dr. Peyton told of the discrimination he endured as a doctor when he moved to Los Angeles. However, his research and clinical work earned him a reputation in

Los Angeles as a specialist in his field. The two men met for lunch and became friends, and together with Joyce's mother, gave us their approval. The biggest obstacle now was my mother, who—once I'd told her how I felt about Joyce, about her beauty and intelligence, about her distinguished family, and that I wanted to marry her—she threatened to kill herself, a cold, hostile, and unbelievable threat on her part. To suit herself, she put herself above my happiness, my love for a woman who did not meet her standards, and my pending marriage.

This wasn't about me; it was about her. I tried to see the issue from her perspective. Why did she discriminate against a black woman? What or who influenced it? Perhaps, when living with her Pasadena relatives, she was influenced by the city's widespread racial discrimination. When I moved to New York, her older sister, Armenouhi, who lived there, told me of her own prejudice against Blacks and hoped that I would not have Black students in my classes. These family attitudes may have helped to shape my mother's thinking. Furthermore, she may have feared our proposed marriage because it would result in a mixed-race grandchild. Despite the fact that Joyce was the beautiful, refined, talented daughter of an important family, my Mother was not interested in having her as a daughter-in-law. To make matters worse, she refused to meet her. The inevitable gossip in Glendale resulting from such a marriage would automatically have wiped out her social status and reputation in the town. Ironically, the Peyton family, as well as the singer Nat King Cole and his family, lived harmoniously in the nearly all-White, gated neighborhood of Hancock Park in Los Angeles. Whatever was influencing her, there was little consideration for me and my future. But I could not explain or change her suicidal threat.

As a result of this tangled situation, Joyce and I made the very painful decision to relinquish our plans. We could have eloped and had a wonderful life, but we respected our parents, even though one of them ruined our plans. We remained in touch after I moved to New York, and twice she visited an aunt who lived in Manhattan, so we saw a little of each other. Back in Los Angeles, she had first become a high school English teacher and then the Principal of a Los Angeles high school in a mixed-race neighborhood, becoming well-known and influential for her educational leadership. Joyce never married. In the early 1980s, she phoned and encouraged me to visit her in L.A., so my partner Edgar and I gladly went. We met for an elegant lunch at the Beverly Wilshire Hotel, and though it was Edgar's and Joyce's only meeting, they quickly became friends with their shared love of art. We continued to talk regularly on the phone. In 1984, a friend of hers called to tell me that Joyce had died from leukemia, something she had kept as a secret from me. I mourned her death, remembering all the good times we had together and those we might have had, but there was nothing I could do except to keep her beautiful spirit in my mind and heart.

Chapter Ten: Coming Out

Homosexuality is Just a Phase

Today, at some time in their lives, in one way or another, most gay people come out of the closet, disclosing their sexual orientation to friends, parents, and family. Yet, it can be a stressful decision at any age or any time. Sixty years ago, when I was 28, I decided to tell my parents that I had been having sex with men for the previous 15 years. Why did I wait so long? Because I figured it wasn't necessary because they knew that I spent more time with men than women, and my mother had too frequently questioned my masculinity. Because she may have heard that two bossy relatives came close to calling me a homo to my face. Because I only mentioned marriage once, and it involved Joyce Peyton.

Thus, I thought that my parents knew my sexual preference and were perhaps among those parents who considered it just a phase in growing up. The word phase was the life raft in which those people believed. "He'll get over it," they'd say, "it's just a phase." It may have been naive on my part to trust in this approach to informing my parents. But it's not a phase. It is a reality that cannot be changed. Now, I was ready to make sure that my parents knew for certain that I was gay. I had yet to decide what, where, why, when, and how I was going to tell them. As you shall soon see, my coming out occurred in an unpredictable way.

My Mother and My Being Gay

My mother was clearly and defiantly an obstacle to my coming out. Since I was ten, she continued to provoke me about my masculinity and my preference for books over football. She never changed this attitude. She did not live to see the results of the gay rights movement, including the happiness that gay freedom, gay marriage, and gay parenthood brought to so many gay couples. Undoubtedly, she worried about what her relatives and neighbors would think if they heard that she had a gay son. Although she knew that Jon and I had shared an apartment and then a house, she may have thought that we were only roommates, not a gay couple. Maybe she was just fooling herself. Now, I was determined to come out. Either she accepted me as gay, or she didn't, yet I remained respectful of her as my mother and unwilling to hurt her. I will not judge her, but seventy years later, this struggle is still in my memory. She wasn't the only parent who could not face the truth.

But her attitude was inconsistent. For example, she and my father were friends with an openly gay couple who lived across the street from them, often having drinks or going out to lunch or dinner with them. She called them the boys. If she accepted them, why couldn't she accept me as another one of the boys? Furthermore, as an artist whose work was displayed and sold in Southern California, she must have encountered many talented gay men and women. She referred to my gay partners, Jon Warner and Edgar Munhall, as her second sons.

What were her expectations of me? Whatever they may have been, I believe I satisfied the professional, if not the personal, ones. My academic achievements at USC should have made her proud. I earned a Ph.D. at the early age of twenty-seven. In 1967, I was appointed an Assistant Professor at CUNY, the country's largest public university. In New York, I worked with my fellow faculty members to establish a new college. After my first two books were published, I received my tenure in 1976, followed shortly by a promotion to full Professor. The college president told me that I was the youngest person in CUNY history ever to reach that status. I don't think that my mother cared about any of this or even believed in the value of intellectual work; perhaps she thought that it would lead nowhere. When I published my first book, which was dedicated to my parents, she said, "Why can't you write something that the neighbors could read?" and "Why don't you go on TV like Gore Vidal and talk about your books?" She died before I had fulfilled my expectations, but up to this time, she showed little pride in my work. I sent my parents copies of all my books, but while my father read some of them, she never even mentioned them.

In 1981, I left teaching to join the CUNY administrative staff, first with an appointment by the Chancellor to the office of University Dean of Faculty and then later as University Dean of Executive Search and Evaluation, which included the presidential searches at CUNY colleges. In 1991, I was chosen to be Provost of Pratt Institute, a private art school in Brooklyn, and after two turbulent years there, I returned to CUNY and the Chancellor's Office, where I was a special assistant, before returning at last to teaching at CUNY's Hunter College. I retired in 2001 at age 63 to write a textbook, Looking at Movies.

Looking back, I may have placed too much emphasis on what my mother thought or would think, but I was raised to love and respect my parents. And, of course, I liked parental recognition. While I knew that my father would not oppose my coming out, I also wanted my mother to accept and live with it. She never did.

Coming Out

It is a sunny Sunday morning in Glendale. I am still in graduate school and living at home. Jon and I were on speaking terms. He was grateful for my parents' viewing him as their second son, as well as their open hospitality, so I expected that he would, as usual, be present for Sunday dinner that evening. I phoned to confirm this, and he said he could not come. I insisted that it was his obligation to be there and that he think twice before hurting my parents' feelings. He hung up the phone without further comment.

I went out and worked in the rose garden. Soon, my father joined me and asked if Jon would be there for dinner. His question, at that moment, was perfectly timed. I knew that he had guessed the strife between Jon and me, and when I told him that Jon wanted to skip dinner that night, he replied, "Where is he?" I had the feeling that he was trying to help me, perhaps to foster a reunion between Jon and me, but I hoped for something more: that he would give me the courage to come out to him. That, in these circumstances, he would understand and support me if I told him that I was gay. So, I did.

I told him that, despite some experiences in having sex with women, I preferred sex with men. Sealing the moment, I said, "I am gay." His astonishing response was, "Do you love him?" I answered, "Not anymore." He replied, "If you love him, you have to fight for him." Then, he told me to call Jon and insist that he come for dinner as part of the family. Jon came, but while this may have pleased my parents, it did nothing to further my fading relationship with him, and in spite of my father's advice, I wasn't going to fight to get him back. It was most important that I had come out to my father, the man I most loved, respected, and trusted.

After this phone call, I returned to the garden and felt that my relationship with my father was strengthened by our frankness with one another. He then told me a part of his past life that I had never heard, an astonishing story that is directly relevant to my feeling confident in coming out to him. He said that, after the Armenian genocide, he was a pre-teen orphan wandering through Turkey in search of comfort, food, shelter, and work. His brother Meran was in New York, and his goal was to contact him and then join him in the U.S.A. Meanwhile, he worked his way toward Constantinople, doing menial farm work to get some food and earn some money. He was careful to avoid farms owned by Turkish people, thinking he was safer at places owned by Bedouin Arabs.

The Bedouins gave him not only work but also food and a place to sleep. However, they also made him pay an unusual price for this care. He was an adolescent boy who knew little or nothing about sex, and he had no choice when they forced him to have anal sex. He endured the ordeal, realizing that it could be a life-or-death issue. So, even though he accepted, he escaped as quickly as he could. He soon reached Constantinople, where he was sheltered at the Roberts College, an Armenian school founded by Americans. The Bedouin sexual experience did not change my father's attitude toward life. He was not surprised when I told him I preferred men. His honesty in telling me this showed that we would always tell each other the truth. In addition, it helped me to find equilibrium in my life. For me, then, coming out was surprisingly easy to do, especially with my father's experience, kindness, and support.

Finishing the Dissertation

I was now free to finish writing my dissertation. Working in my former bedroom in the house where I grew up, with its view of the garden and mountains behind, made for a peaceful and quiet time in which to work. The purpose of a dissertation is to demonstrate that the Ph.D. candidate has learned the methods necessary for researching and writing a long essay on a single subject. One of my areas of specialization was the English drama of the Restoration era (1660 to 1710). Although I preferred the wonderful comedies of that period, there was a better opportunity for writing my essay on the tragedies, so I chose Cambyses, King of Persia (1675) by Elkanah Settle. This playwright's work—including tragedies, a comedy, two operas, and many poems—was very popular in London, on and off the stage, so popular, even notorious, that Settle was considered a rival to John Dryden, who at the time was the Poet Laureate. In 1691, Settle was named London City Poet, but today, he is known chiefly by scholars of Restoration literature.

The text of Cambyses, his most famous play, appeared in four different editions, each running at one time or another on the London stage. Although the history of Restoration drama has been deeply studied and recorded in scholarly books, Settle never specified which version of the play was his favorite, the version he wanted to be remembered by, so my task was to establish that. It proved to be a challenge, but the task was made easier through the generosity of Charlton Hinman, a scholar who invented the Hinman collator, an optical device compared these four editions and displayed the differences in the texts. At that time, it was my good luck that Hinman was doing research at the Huntington Library at the same time I was, and when he learned of my project, he graciously gave me access to his own machine.

My parents supported this work, and so I explained each stage of my progress so they wouldn't feel left out of this important moment in my life. I did my most relevant study at two local libraries: the Huntington Library in San Marino, one of the world's great rare book libraries, and the William Andrews Clark Library in West Los Angeles, whose collection of 18th-century books and manuscripts in Restoration drama was invaluable. After I produced a rough draft manuscript, I spent hours editing, rewriting, and typing it on my rented IBM electric typewriter. When I completed writing it, I had it professionally typed. Then, all that was left to fulfill the degree requirements was passing four exams on my areas of specialization, each lasting four hours, and an oral defense of the dissertation to my faculty committee.

Working at home included some of the best times I ever had with my parents. I would sometimes work until the early morning hours and then sneak downstairs to make a pizza, the ingredients for which my mother had already laid out. When she heard me in the kitchen, she came down to join me in having a nightcap and a slice of pizza.

Finally, at the June 1967 graduation ceremonies, USC President Norman Topping handed me the diploma granting me a Ph.D. We shook hands, and as I proceeded off the stage, Topping called out, "Wait, Dr. Barsam. Come back." He then told the audience that at 27 years, I was the youngest person to receive a doctoral degree in USC's 87-year history. Applause. He then turned to me and said, "Well, what do you think of that?" Stunned, I held up the diploma and said "I thought you were going to take it back" which got a good laugh from the audience. That evening, my parents hosted a party at home for my friends, including Jon.

Preparing for the Move to New York

I was ready now to move to a new life in New York City: new environment, job, colleagues, friends, and experiences. I cannot say that my parents were excited about this, but they nonetheless supported it. Although I had spent several weeks there in the summer of 1964, this was for keeps. I replaced my Austin-Healey with a yellow Volkswagen convertible, shipped my belongings to New York, and then took a leisurely driving trip across the country. In helping me to pack, my mother gave me a few items that reflected her feelings about me: a folder of recipes for my favorite food so that I might cook them, a very useful sewing kit for when I needed to sew on a button, and an album of family photographs up till the present time. I was astonished, bewildered, and offended to see that she had carefully scissored her face out of all the photos. A psychologist told me that such behavior is a form of narcissism, a familiar mother-son situation in which the mother lacks empathy for the son and may deliberately create tension between them. I did not save the album, but I never forgot it.

During this time, I taught a night-time literature class at Glendale Community College. One of my older students was Susan Nevins, who was an engineer in the U. S. inter-planetary and deep space flight programs at the NASA Jet Propulsion Laboratory in nearby Pasadena. We became friends, had drinks or dinner together, and revealed the following coincidence. When I told her that I would soon be moving to New York, she told me that she was also moving to take a new position at the NASA Goddard Space Flight Center in Maryland. Since we were both going in the same direction at the same time, I invited her to join me in the VW for the journey East. I did the driving, and we shared the cost of the gas. We stopped at several national parks and monuments, enjoyed all kinds of restaurants, stayed in motels (two bedrooms), and, in total, had a marvelous time together. I delivered her to her new residence in Maryland, where she would begin her new life; I headed up to New York to begin mine.

Chapter Eleven:
Manhattan And Me: Part One

1967-1991

In her short story, "The Sculptor's Funeral," Willa Cather wrote that Sand City, Kansas, was—at the turn of the 19th century—a "dead little Western town . . . a little world of small-minded gossip and proud ignorance." She could as easily have been writing about Glendale in my early years. Cather spent her early years in Red Cloud, Nebraska, whose people she loved and whose lives she often wrote about. At twenty-three, she moved to Pittsburgh, and then ten years later, to New York City, which remained her home for the rest of her life. As I was attracted to men, she was to women. I learned from my faithful reading of The New Yorker that Manhattan was the country's most cosmopolitan city. Later, after I moved there, I learned from experience that it has something for everyone and room for everyone, and thus provides unlimited opportunities for a person like me to grow.

My first trip to New York City, in the Summer of 1964, was a short vacation organized by Gary Meadows, who was already living and working there. He knew the city very well and introduced me to its museums, opera houses, theaters, restaurants, neighborhoods, and parks. This included a week at Fire Island Pines, a summer playground for gay New Yorkers. The Pines attracted a variety of people: young, handsome men in their early twenties, many with good jobs in fashion, who liked the wild lifestyle of liquor, drugs, and sex; older men, wealthy and retired, who founded the place, made its history, and owned their own homes; and finally the newcomers, not knowing what to expect and testing the waters. Since the surf there had a dangerous undertow, many homes had swimming pools. It was the golden age of the Pines.

A typical weekend trip started with a three-hour chartered bus ride to the town of Sayville on Long Island followed by a short ferry ride to Fire Island. People who could afford it chartered seaplanes that flew from Manhattan straight to the Pines dock. On departing the ferry, we were dazzled by young guys wearing as little as possible to show off their well-toned bodies. Later in the afternoon, we'd see a similar crowd at the tea dance, a ritual that took place in the principal bar. Of course, there were other summer residents, like clothes tycoon Calvin Klein, the photographer Robert Mapplethorpe, and Truman Capote, who said he wrote Breakfast at Tiffany's there. There were film stars too. Walking one day on the boardwalk, I stopped to help a woman who had dropped a grocery bag; when she looked up, I met Claudette Colbert. Twenty-four hours a day, guys wandered off that boardwalk and into the woods, known as the "meat rack," where all kinds of sex were going on out in the open. AIDS had not yet emerged as a menace. The place was a clique of regulars who went every weekend. Since we were not recognized as a part of that crowd, we were only invited to a few parties.

Even though we had very different tastes in people, Gary introduced me to people he thought I would like. Indeed, he tried to manage all aspects of my new life. He didn't much like David Roggensack, whom I met in the Pines, and became my first New York boyfriend. He was two years older than me, Iowa-born, and with a sensible Midwestern outlook on life. He taught me a lot about how to navigate and behave in the gay world, even introducing me to some of his friends. David, who was a Broadway press representative, used his press pass to get free tickets to many shows. For my 29th birthday in 1967, David took me to see "Illya Darling," a stage adaptation of the film "Never on Sunday," both starring the exciting Greek actor, Melina Mercouri. During the curtain calls, Miss Mercouri came towards the footlights, saying "Opa" (equivalent to "wow") over and over, then blew a kiss to me, and with that million-dollar smile, said "Happy birthday Richard" loud enough so the audience could hear her. The audience picked up on this and yelled "Happy birthday" to me. Of course, David arranged it. He was always doing nice things like that for me, and while he wanted us to share an apartment, I wasn't ready for any serious relationship at that time. However, he remained in my circle of friends for the next few years. Aside from writing press releases, he aspired to be a more serious writer and sent me ideas for books he was trying to write, asking for my opinion. I must have offended him when I told him I was too busy with my own writing to help him. However, David persisted, and at a time when roller skating had a revival in the city, he not only proved to be a champion skater but also the author The Wonderful World of Roller

Skating. We lost contact after he retired and moved upstate with his new boyfriend.

Enter Upper Stage, Erica Bell

About this time, I met Erica Bell, who is not only my lawyer but also a person with whom I share a very special friendship. She was born and raised in Greenwich Village, one of two girls and a boy, and gets her interest in all of arts from contacts there as well as from being distantly related to James Agee. In 1973, she met Murray, a self-proclaimed "Bronx girl," who, after graduate school, taught English in a variety of settings, including a night school for hospital workers. Erica and Gail married in 2011 and remained happily together for more than 50 years. The two things she loved the most were cooking, at which she was superb, and visiting Italy, where she felt more at home than anywhere else. I only wish I had met her earlier and got to know her better, for, alas, she died in 2024 from brain cancer at age 72. She sold her law practice to another firm, yet remains the attorney for many in the gay community.

Erica enjoyed this story from my travels. Edgar and I had rented a summer house in Aix-en-Provence, to which I invited my friend Renata (not her real name) to spend a week with us. She is an avid opera fan, and Aix has a summer program of all types of opera, from Puccini to the most modern. I thought she would enjoy attending some of them. The house was large, and she was not an easy person to share it with, and she soon began to complain. Her bedroom was too far from the bathroom; the noise of the city kept her awake; she didn't like the food, and she showed no interest whatsoever in the opera being offered. One morning, instead of having breakfast with us, she said she was going for a walk. Later, when we embarked on a planned driving trip through the countryside, she sat in the back seat, took out a bag from the local bakery, and began to eat a croissant. We always had them on the breakfast table, but she pointed out that hers were from a better bakery. After the first croissant, she ate another, and then another, and then the fourth. I was driving, of course, and Edgar was in the passenger seat, and we did not comment. Later, he made an exaggerated caricature of Renata for his drawing book, depicting her devouring croissants. He labeled it "Miss Piggy." As was his custom with such drawings, and as a man who respected his friends, he never showed it to the victim. When I showed Erica the drawing, she could not stop laughing, so I had a framed reproduction made for her.

Gary Meadows was obsessed by the celebrities who made New York exciting, and, through him, I met such gay men as Montgomery Clift, Bill Blass, and Edward Albee. It was at Albee's Montauk retreat, where we had been invited for a weekend, that I met his neighbor John Steinbeck and his wife at dinner. The great writer was so shy that he almost did not come, but he did, and we all enjoyed a memorable meal cooked by Albee. Gary never had a gay partner and said he never wanted one. I was his closest friend. He did not approve of my desire to meet the right man for a relationship. So when in 1977, I became Edgar Munhall's partner, Gary dropped me. Call it envy, whatever, but he had lost control over me. He made his own life in the gay underworld of leather bars and steam baths. He was successful as a senior editor at McGraw-Hill but careless in his private life and died from AIDS in 1980.

My Mother's Visit

My mother's sister, Armenouhi Pashgian, lived in New York, and though they corresponded by letter, the two hadn't seen each other for some time, but when my aunt was in failing health, my mother came to stay with me and to visit her. Aunt Armen, with whom I enjoyed visiting, had worked as secretary to the stage director, Rouben Mamoulian. On the day Mother was going to visit her sister, she asked that I call after she had spent an hour. I could tell immediately that the visit made her very uncomfortable to the point where, outside my aunt's house, she took medicine for a heart problem. She did not make another visit. I did not really understand the deeper aspects of the relationship between the two women. They were never close, and aside from one trip to California, her sister remained in New York and my mother in Glendale.

From the first hour of her stay with me, she complained about the apartment. The noise of the toilet flushing in the apartment above annoyed her. The kitchen was too small (it was). When I brought bagels and cream cheese for breakfast, she got angry for some reason and wouldn't touch them. Unfortunately, she made a negative remark about Jewish food. She nagged me about not wanting to marry. She showed little or no interest in the college where I taught and was cool about the academic book I was then writing. We went to the theater, and she did enjoy the performance by Ingrid Bergman, but during most of her stay she was in a black mood. To top it off, she asked me to change her return ticket so that she could fly back to Glendale at the first opportunity.

I was happy in New York, having freed myself from her negative feelings about it, and found my own world here. It's all about finding a place and being accepted there for what you are, not what someone else wants you to be. And I took her as she was, and in no way would I think about changing my life or where I lived it. We kept in close touch. I was 3,000 miles away and wrote to her frequently because phone calls in those days were expensive. While she and my father returned together several times to visit me, and I almost annually visited them, this was her only solo visit. My father loved New York, and he returned several times by himself after her death.

Richmond College

Before moving to Manhattan, I applied for teaching jobs in local colleges. Following the interviews and offers from three colleges, I scored a position as assistant professor of English Literature at Richmond College of the City University of New York (CUNY). When most people unfamiliar with New York City hear the name CUNY, they think only of City College (CCNY), founded in 1847 as the Free Academy, an institution offering underprivileged students the opportunity for advanced study. That has remained its mission ever since. CUNY is separate from SUNY, the State University of New York.

CUNY was created as an administrative structure to consolidate New York City's many institutions of high education under one authority. It is today the nation's leading urban public university, comprising twenty-five institutions: eleven senior colleges, seven community colleges, an Honors College, Graduate Center for Ph.D. candidates, a Graduate School of Journalism, a School of Labor and Urban Studies, a School of Law, a School of Professional Studies, and a Graduate School of Public Health and Health Policy. The University serves more than 200,000 degree-seeking students each year.

In 1967, Richmond College existed only on paper. I was hired along with seventy other young people who, like me, were chosen to create this new college from the ground up, a venture underwritten by the Carnegie Foundation. Many of my colleagues had doctoral degrees from such Eastern colleges as Harvard, Yale, Pennsylvania, and Columbia. Only two of us came from a Western school, one from the University of California at Berkeley and me from USC. Our collective job as charter faculty members was to establish the curriculum, course requirements, the courses themselves, and college-wide grading standards. Most of us had a traditional college education and now believed that our future students needed a fresh, different educational experience. We were not radicals, just revolutionaries. We would begin to teach when the college opened in September.

We were all newly minted academics. Many of them were aloof, distancing themselves from forming friendships outside of the college while presenting themselves as intellectuals at work. Karl Marx seemed to enter every discussion. They tried to outtalk each other, with some making attempts to dress a certain way, smoke a pipe instead of cigarettes, and sit in the cafeteria not with colleagues but with a book. They wanted to appear immersed in their work, central casting intellectuals. Fortunately, the female colleagues were more secure and often took on leadership roles. I refer to people in their early thirties who were not yet settled in their academic positions, not yet publishing articles or books, and honestly, like me, rather unsure of their direction. Moreover, we were all learning how to be teachers. It was a contest of education and knowledge. I greatly enjoyed watching my colleagues participate in this game.

Richmond College would be neither a community college for students who wanted a two-year academic program in career fields, nor a four-year college that offered an education leading to a Bachelor's degree, but a combination of both. Four out of five of the New York City boroughs had at least one community and one senior college, but Staten Island had only Staten Island Community College (SICC), which had an outstanding national reputation. Staten Island politicians had long wanted a senior college that would offer their children, without leaving the island, accessibility to the same level of higher education enjoyed by students in the other boroughs. Richmond College would help to make that possible.

Our goal, then, was to develop the last two years of baccalaureate programs so that SICC students could transfer and finish their college education in their home borough. SICC would remain on its current campus, and the new senior college would, for its first years, occupy a new building a short walk from the ferry terminal. Since nearly all the new faculty lived in Manhattan—that's why we moved here—the ferry was our daily shuttle. When we began to meet the challenge for which we were hired, we didn't know—and this is essential information—that the CUNY administration was quietly planning to merge these two separate institutions into what was finally named The College of Staten Island. Mergers in higher education, such as this one, were very rare in the United States. If two institutions cooperate, it might work, but when it is politically motivated and forced on faculty and staff, all sorts of problems arise. The major issue is merging two faculty groups, each with its different credentials and institutional expectations for teaching and promotion. One group is trained to offer introductory and secondary-level classes in certain fields, while the other is qualified to teach classes in a liberal arts curriculum. At CUNY, faculty in the first group are not required to have a Ph.D., but faculty in the second group must have received a Ph.D. before their initial appointment. A faculty union ensures equal representation and benefits for both groups.

To some people, this would seem to be an impossible undertaking, but we were hired to do it, paid our full teaching salaries for the first year, and determined to finish our work by September. The Chancellor's office had already appointed the principal administrators—President, Deans, and Division Chairs—with whom we worked regularly throughout the summer months. We hoped to attract an unusually talented first group of students, an effort for which CUNY conducted a wide recruitment effort targeting students from colleges in the Northeast states, encouraging them to apply. Those selected for admission would be eligible by having finished the first two years of a liberal arts curriculum in their majors and earning a B grade point average.

Jeffrey Burke, the type of student we wanted, was studying at LeMoyne College, a Jesuit institution upstate, the product of a strict Jesuit education. But he left it when, two years later, he learned that Richmond College was recruiting students who wanted a different kind of teaching and learning, where the student, not the priest or professor, was the most important person in the classroom. And where total fees were less than $100 per annum! I met him while teaching my first classes at Richmond. He shined like a star, reading everything from British Restoration comedies to Joyce's Ulysses with insight and understanding as yet unknown to many of his classmates.

While in college, Jeffrey lived with his family in an apartment near mine, so we frequently got together for conversation over a few beers, a habit that continued after he graduated from Richmond. Next, while attending the CUNY Graduate Center, he landed his first job in publishing at Harper's Magazine, a venerable monthly publication that featured articles and essays on everything from literature to politics and the arts. Its editor at the time, Lewis Lapham, became Jeffrey's mentor. Jeff went on to work as a news editor at the Wall Street Journal, a senior editor at Vanity Fair magazine, and eventually a page-one editor for the Asian, European and U.S. editions of the WSJ for some 25 years, where he worked for years on the U.S. edition until being sent to Hong Kong to work on the Asian edition. There, he met and married Antje, with whom he had two daughters before they returned to the U.S.A. where he continued to work at the WSJ and then for the Bloomberg News and REDD Financial Newswire. After retiring to Wilmington, North Carolina, he took on reviewing fiction for Kirkus magazine and The Guardian in London. In his free time, he and his wife kayak on the backwaters and play Pickleball with the neighbors. We have maintained contact for the 51 years since Richmond College, and I am proud to have been something of a mentor to him and delighted to have him as a witty and loyal friend.

As summer came to an end, the Richmond faculty had created a liberal arts curriculum divided into four divisions: Humanities, Social Sciences, Physical Sciences, and Teacher Education. We wrote course descriptions, specified that enrollment in some classes would be limited to fifteen, and, whenever appropriate, conducted as seminars. Reading lists, as well as writing assignments, would be substantial, and students were to be graded on a system of three grades: Honors, Passing, and Not Passing. We worked closely with the deans of the four academic divisions, whereas we very rarely met with the President. He was a professor of higher education near retirement at City College, clearly uncomfortable with our youthful vitality and the new college we were creating. He was not the man for the job, and he proved it.

At the end of our first academic year, both faculty and students agreed that our college was stable. However, the Vietnam War deeply engaged college students in campus protests. Sit-ins resulted in canceled classes and a general state of confusion, but the faculty was engaged and supportive. A small Hippie counterculture grew within this turmoil, one built on drugs, rock music, sexual liberation, and a lack of trust in anyone over thirty. And while almost all students were engaged in protests, they also managed to complete their academic work. Within the overall student population, there was a group concerned with the rights of women and gays, among the first to raise these issues in the academic world. Some Hippies came to class high on grass and accompanied by a stray dog on a quickly fashioned leash. Students seemed to care for everybody and everything.

Students in my classes demonstrated a genuine desire to learn within the principles of our experimental college. In that first year, I taught courses in English literature of the 18th and the 20th centuries, with a particular emphasis on the latter. It was no surprise that students were more interested in the modern than the ancient, yet my classes in 18th-century literature were always lively. However, my most popular course among students was the one devoted to the works of James Joyce, primarily the reading of Ulysses. Considering the complexity of the novel and the intensity with which we studied it, I knew that these were exceptional students. It became one of the most popular courses in the college.

Mark Berman: Part One

Another student, Mark Berman, was also devoted to reading Joyce and impressed me with his willingness to get into vigorous arguments about the novel. His former education, like Burke's, was in a religious setting, a Hebrew Yeshiva on Long Island. During the

1967 holiday season, Mark was on holiday in Florida with his family, which he interrupted by returning to New York. I was quite surprised when he rang my doorbell, asked to come in, put his suitcase down, and said he was in love with me. At first, I thought this was just the familiar crush of a student on a favorite teacher. He told me that he came from a wealthy family, that he had an over-protective mother, and was determined to lead a free life away from home. One thing led to another and he moved in with me.

Mark was kind, gentle, and exceptionally handsome, yet inexperienced in life. He had his first gay sexual experience with me. I told him that having an affair with a student could ruin my career and asked him to keep ours a secret until he graduated at the end of the year. He handled that challenge with style. He then began working toward an advanced degree in art history at the CUNY Graduate Center. In the meantime, we happily stayed together and remained living with me for several years before he moved to his own apartment.

One of the great benefits of college life is that faculty and students have three months every summer to do what they want. Mark and I spent several of those summers traveling in Europe. He bought a new car, which was delivered in London, and we exchanged driving duties, touring England, France, Germany, Belgium, Spain, and Italy, enjoying museums and great restaurants. One year, we rented a summer house in Todi, a small hill town in Umbria. The house, located on a large farm, faced the river Tiber, which, being placid at that point, was good for swimming. I spent mornings working on a book about Ulysses, and in the afternoons, we drove around the countryside, visiting the little towns, their markets, and churches and returning to the house with a car full of fresh vegetables and fruit.

We remained lovers, but after we returned to New York from Italy, Mark, who was twelve years younger than I, got restless and wanted to experience the gay world beyond our relationship. He put a hold on his schoolwork and went to Rome, supposedly to study Italian painting. Instead, he became involved with Baron Brian de Breffny, a much older man. From what I knew him from meeting him previously, I knew he would endanger our relationship. Despite his questionable title, he was born Brian Michael Lees in Ireland—a country free of any pretensions to having an aristocracy or noble titles—yet he had created a title for himself. Breffny earned his living by creating expensive coffee-table books of photographs, many devoted to Ireland. In Rome, he lived in an apartment with two Indian servants and moved in a circle of celebrities, including author Muriel Spark, his best friend, who took Mark into her circle of gay men. Mark enjoyed life with them but nonetheless wrote to me every week and always ended by saying he loved me. When he returned to New York to spend short visits, he was still unsure of whom he loved, the phony aristocrat or me. Against my advice, he returned to Rome without finishing his graduate studies. He will re-enter my life soon.

Skiing in France

In 1971, I decided to take advantage of the Winter Break and go skiing in France. Several years before, I learned to ski at Mammoth

Mountain, California and later worked further on my ability at Alta, Utah. I believed I was ready for the French Alpine ski trails, and I chose Megève, a small city in the Auvergne-Rhône-Alpes region in Southeastern France, easily reached by plane from New York. Near Mont Blanc in the French Alps, it is best known as a ski resort that the Rothschilds built as a French alternative to St. Moritz in Switzerland. It regained its reputation for wealthy skiers and high prices, but there was always room for the rest of us. I arrived the day after Christmas and planned to stay for two weeks. I booked a room with a balcony in a mid-priced pension that included all meals in the price. They took very good care of me, and I was able to use my years of studying French to mingle successfully with the other guests. The first day of my trip was spent getting acquainted with the town and buying my pass to gain access to the chair lifts and the skiing trails. I quickly learned that the prices of almost everything in Megève were high. Walking through the charming town, I tried to feel that I belonged there, which, as a skier, I guess I did. On the second day, I woke early, had a hearty breakfast, went to the entrance to the slopes, and scanned my entry pass. A computer electronically records the name and number of a skier's information for his protection. The trails themselves are well-patrolled and guarded by the ski patrol. At the end of the day, they examine the records to determine if everyone has left by the required deadline. If someone appears to remain on the slopes, the ski patrol already knows the age and gender of the person and begins a search.

In mid-afternoon, I chose an intermediate trail to end my day. It was steep enough to be a challenge but not sufficient to be forbidding, and I got a good start. I was the only skier on my trail, so I enjoyed myself until I saw a young skier going very fast downhill on a prohibited trail to my right. As it happened, she illegally crossed directly in front of me, her skis catching me underneath and flipping me into the air. I came down hard on my shoulders. She disappeared down the slope, but I was able to help somewhat by raising the skis and standing them vertically in the snow, a sign of trouble that I knew the ski patrol would eventually see. As the day grew darker, I lost track of time and place.

Eventually, the ski patrol found me and put me on a temporary stretcher attached to a snowplow that dragged me up the mountain to one of the rest and refreshment cottages. It was very cold inside, so they laid me on the floor and brought a large St. Bernard dog to lie down beside me and provide some warmth. It was almost comic, yet the dog and I easily snuggled together. An hour passed before an ambulance arrived. By then, not having received any medication, I was in great pain and, due to some head injuries, was going in and out of consciousness. Later, in the hospital, I was told that my left collarbone was broken and would require surgery to repair it.

The local police, working with the ski patrol team, helped me to identify the person who had caused my accident. After studying the electronic records of late afternoon departures from the slopes, they identified, without a doubt, a fourteen-year-old girl as the guilty party. In the meantime, I was getting settled in the hospital, had dinner, and did not learn about her until the following day. The police told me that the girl was very distressed as she told her side of the story. They gave her and her parents a summons to appear the next day before a judge who handled the law pertaining to skiing. Since she was a minor, she couldn't be arrested, but the judge gave her the severest penalty he could: to forbid the girl to use all ski facilities in France for the remainder of her life. That may sound harsh, but she could easily have killed me, considering the angle and speed of her stupid and careless action. Her parents were liable for all costs involved in my hospitalization and return airfare.

The surgery went well, but the hospital required me to spend ten days recuperating before leaving. The doctor said I might need further surgery when I saw my doctor in New York. After they appeared in court, the girl and her mother visited me, bringing flowers and chocolates. The girl was remorseful and tearfully begged me to forgive her. I told her that I was sorry for her but couldn't forgive her, for her actions caused me severe pain before and after surgery and ruined my trip. To make the situation worse, my orthopedic doctor in New York said that I would need more surgery to re-break the collar bone and set it properly.

Several years later, I returned to France and skiing at Courchevel. Edgar came with me, and I arranged some ski lessons for him, but he decided against it after visiting the slopes, saying in his inimitable manner, "You expect me to spend my week with people who dress like that?" He was concerned that he might be injured, as I was in Megève. Although he rejected skiing, he spent a pleasant week reading and swimming at the hotel at the foot of Mt. Blanc. This ended my skiing career. Ten days after he flew back to his job in New York, I was taken. on a stretcher from the hospital to the Megève airport, put on a first-class seat converted to a bed, and flew home. That was the end of my skiing career.

Chapter Twelve:
Manhattan And Me: Part Two

Bobby Short Enters My Life

I first met Bobby Short, then a star of New York's cabaret world, when I was a freshman at USC. Bobby was there for his annual engagement at The Haig, the best-known nightclub in town, a tiny place located across from the Ambassador Hotel. All the country's notable jazz artists played there. When I went to hear him, I was not yet of drinking age, so I was not permitted to enter. When I promised to drink only Coke, the manager conceded. He must have told Bobby that an ardent fan was in the audience because, during his break, Mr. Short came to my table. We talked about his work and my studies, and eventually, he invited me to visit him when I was in New York. So when I went there for my first visit in 1964 to see Gary Meadows, I told him about Bobby, and Gary said he already knew him and would ask him to arrange a meeting. The three of us spent several days together, including a memorable visit to the Bronx Zoo, where Bobby wanted to see the rare snow leopards.

Now, in 1967, when I had settled in New York, Bobby re-entered my life. Why did I find him so appealing? I was attracted primarily to his great talent, his presence both on stage and off, and his kindness to everyone. I liked his friends, the restaurants he chose, and his overall style of living. Even though he was a first-class star, he was likely, when in certain situations, to be insecure about race. I remember an incident when we were in a NYC taxicab, and the driver, who recognized him, made a remark that insulted Blacks. Bobby told him to pull over to the curb, and we got out and walked. I was proud of the way handled it and not provoking the driver. As for why I appealed to him, I think he was interested in my education and career, so different from his background, and often proudly introduced me as Professor Barsam.

He had since moved from his Carnegie Hall studio apartment to the legendary Osborne apartment house across 57th Street, where he bought a large apartment from Leonard Bernstein. It consisted of a living room, dining room, five bedrooms, each with a working fireplace, a grand kitchen, and servant's quarters. Bobby's success was as good as it gets. He was from a poor kid from Illinois who worked his way up in show business with his own act, with help from Duke Ellington and other jazz stars, and who some years later became the star performer at the Café bar and nightclub in the Hotel Carlyle. Like Frank Sinatra, he referred to himself as a "saloon singer," and without a doubt, the Café Carlyle was the most luxurious saloon in town.

Since I lived on East 76th Street near the Carlyle, I got my next day's class lecture ready and then rode my bike there and watched his last show. When we were alone, Bobby and I easily warmed to one another, but he was wary of relationships chiefly because he was afraid of coming out publicly as gay, something that very few performers did in those days. He dated women to keep up his public reputation, and at one time, he and Gloria Vanderbilt planned to marry. However, we made no secret of our affection for one another, and he took me everywhere he went, for lunch, shopping, or a movie. We had what I would call a romantic friendship, but not a love affair. Nevertheless, he was very possessive of me and jealous of anything I did without him.

Bobby was a great biker. He often rode his bicycle to the Carlyle, and we rode together in Central Park. After his show, we would go out for a snack and then back to the Osborne, where I spent the night. Celebrities were often at his show, including Lauren Bacall and her husband, Jason Robards, Jr. They invited Bobby and Me to join them for a hamburger at P. J. Clarke's, the famous bar and eatery. Although it closed around 1 A.M., the owner gave Bacall and other celebrities a key to the front door to be used after that time. The key gave her gratis access to the bar and kitchen, including food and drink. She made excellent hamburgers, and after a chummy evening, we all went home at 3 A.M. Bobby always referred to friends as his chums.

Before leaving, I gently asked Bacall if she remembered that we'd met years before on the deck of the "Santana" after I escaped a shark attack. She seemed to recall it, but quickly changed the subject. Several years later at Balducci's food emporium in Greenwich Village, she and I were standing close to each other at a food counter, trying to decide what to buy. Perhaps I gazed at her too boldly or too long, for she turned and snarled: "What's the matter, kid? You never saw a movie star before?" She had clearly been drinking that afternoon but changed from her snarl to, "Don't I know you?" This kid again reminded her of our night at P. J. Clarkes as well as our Catalina Island meeting, but she seemed reluctant to talk, so I just said farewell and walked away.

By this time, Bobby was at the height of his career, filling the Café Carlyle every night. His chums, indeed, his clique, were his age or older, nearly all of them White gay men involved in the entertainment business or investing in it. Two of them were Texas millionaires. And as with the coterie that surrounds most celebrities, they were protective of their idol, suspicious of outsiders or newcomers. Bobby held me close to him, literally and figuratively, which made it clear that I was also a chum.

We also had a larger group of admirers and personal friends who were members of what was then called high society. They were White, of course, and basked in his presence at their cocktail parties. Because he was free on Sunday nights, Bobby loved to entertain at Sunday luncheons. Bobby and I helped his houseman, who did most of the cooking. I can remember him teaching me the proper way to make pig's feet, a Southern delight that he often served friends. He made sure there was enough Dom Perignon champagne to keep us all happy. Two of the regular guests whom I particularly enjoyed seeing were Mabel Mercer, who, along with Bobby, was regarded as the foremost interpreter of Cole Porter's songs, and at the other end of the musical spectrum, Jessye Norman, an opera singer known throughout the world. Mabel liked to talk about the horses she had at her country house, and I advised Jessye, who had moved near me on the Upper East Side, where to find the best butcher in the neighborhood. Another of Bobby's guests was the vivacious and beautiful Nan Kempner, who was regularly judged one of the world's best-dressed women. If she were sitting next to you at a table, she would steal bites from your plate. She and often had lunch together at Mortimer's, then a society watering hole that also attracted the fashion crowd, including such regulars as Bill Blass and Oscar de la Renta. Nan, literally the queen of that crowd, had lunch there almost every day.

Bobby and I took pleasure trips together. We were in St. Bart's before it became wildly popular, and where I tried to teach him how to swim, but he never learned because he was afraid of the deep water. Our return flight to New York stopped at another island to pick up more passengers, and then it was canceled. We left the plane to find the small airport jammed with people in the same situation. All the seats were taken, so we spread out some newspapers and joined a lot of others on the floor. A few minutes later, who should appear but Benny Goodman, a good friend of Bobby's, who he took us with him into the lounge reserved for first-class travelers. Goodman was not only the greatest of jazz musicians but also one of the nicest and most modest people I've ever met.

On a wonderful trip to London, we looked up Bobby's friend, actor Charles Gray, who lived in an apartment next to Ava Gardner's. Bobby and I wanted to meet her, so Gray arranged that. Alas, she was another star whose career was troubled with alcoholism, and when she greeted us, I could see that it had almost ruined her beauty. Nevertheless, she was a charming hostess. Also, on that trip, we had dinner at the apartment of fashion designer Jean Muir. Her husband had installed a unit that projected color photographs of beautiful places onto the four walls, which made you feel like you were eating in Portofino rather than in a Mayfair dining room, not that there was anything wrong with the food or the dining room.

And when good food and "fine dining" were becoming very popular in New York, no one was more responsible for that than Craig Claiborne, the popular food critic and editor of The New York Times. He invited Bobby and me to spend a weekend at his Hamptons house. Craig was another heavy drinker, but it did not hamper his abilities in the kitchen. When I told him that I liked to cook and would be happy to help him in the kitchen, he gave me an apron and some tasks. He had planned a dinner of homemade German sausages and all that went with them and taught me how to "feed" the sausage grinder and then seal the chopped meat into an edible sheath. He did the cooking. At dinner, we were joined by his neighbor Pierre Franey, an equally famous gourmet chef, television personality, and author of cookbooks. Pierre's wife stayed at home that night, which made it very easy for Craig to demonstrate the passionate but useless crush he had on Pierre.

Throughout his career, Bobby continually expressed his gratitude to Duke Ellington, who had a great influence on his early development as a singer and throughout his career. To honor his patron, Bobby championed a project to erect a memorial to his mentor. He was tireless in raising the necessary funds. It was dedicated in 1997 and placed just beyond the Northeastern end of Central Park, and if you stand beneath it—it is on ten-foot columns—

you will see a greater-than-life-size bronze statue of Ellington standing next to a piano overlooking Harlem.

Bobby's schedule included an annual concert with the Boston Symphony Pops Orchestra, as well as more intimate performances at private parties and weddings. He insisted that I accompany him on these gigs so long as it didn't interfere with my teaching schedule. In Texas Bobby was scheduled to sing at a wedding party of the daughter of one of his closest women friends. I went along; we were refused pre-booked rooms at a local hotel because two of the party were Black, Bobby and Beverly Peer, his bass fiddler. Our hostess came and took us back to her house, where we spent the night. The next morning, she went into town, bought the hotel, and had it closed down and torn down. When we went to Europe, not for work but for pleasure, there was always somebody in Paris or Venice who gave a party for him at which he would sing a song or two. If it were a small, intimate gathering of people who knew us both, he would end with George Gershwin's Somebody Loves Me, saying, "This one's for Richard."

But Bobby could be unpredictable with his emotions, and didn't give me the stability I wanted in our relationship. However, we remained chums for several years until I told him I had begun seeing Edgar Munhall. He said that he knew Edgar from performances he had given at Frick parties and that he seemed to be someone who would give me the partnership I wanted. Which is exactly what happened. Bobby and I kept in touch, for I sent him copies of my books and sometimes dropped in alone at the Carlyle for old-time's sake. He was gracious, as always, and happy to see me. By 2004, he was in ill health, his career at an end. He died from leukemia in 2005 at the age of 80. A memorial plaque, placed by NewYork City's Mayor on the wall outside wall of the Café Carlyle, reads Bobby Short Place.

Richmond College becomes The College of Staten Island

In 1975, Mayor Abe Beame declared that New York City was bankrupt and had been forced to hand over the city's financial management to New York State. An attempt to secure federal aid from President Ford led to a notorious headline in the Daily News: "FORD TO CITY: DROP DEAD." The entire city faced unpredictable changes as it approached the ensuing chaos. Given the magnitude of the problem, the future of Richmond College was merely a small issue in this larger context. Despite loud protests from CUNY's faculty and students, the future meant significant cuts to the city budget.

CUNY, which has been funded almost entirely by city resources and remained tuition-free since its establishment, was mandated by New York State to charge tuition for all students. This decision significantly altered the university's mission and led to a decrease in future student admissions. In 1976, the University was also instructed to merge SICC and RC into a new institution called The College of Staten Island. The new president, Edmund Volpe, a former English professor at CCNY, held prestige in his position but struggled to manage the turmoil that the new institution faced, which persisted for the next decade.

As I have noted, the merger of academic institutions is seldom successful. Neither SICC nor RC was favorable to this merger, yet City Hall pressured the CUNY Board of Trustees to approve it. This forced decision worked for some, but not all. Indeed, the merger changed the professional lives of those of us who created the college. It not only sullied our dignity and betrayed the employment contract we had signed but also devalued our accomplishments to date in research, teaching, and publishing. It also meant that the dream of our new college was dead, crushed by politicians who knew little about higher education. We were not alone, however, for the newly named college was just one part of the larger New York City community that suffered deeply because of New York City and State financial troubles.

The College of Staten Island

The new college made significant progress not only in attracting students and faculty but also in expanding the courses and degrees offered. The Dean, recognizing my background as both a film historian and an English Lit professor, inquired whether I would be interested in developing a degree-granting film program, collaborating with Gerald Mast, another faculty member keen on integrating cinema into the academic curriculum. Gerald had already published A Short History of the Movies, and my first book, Nonfiction Film: A Critical History, came out in 1973. Working together, we launched a B.A. program in Cinema Studies within a year, which attracted a large group of students, and established an M.A. four years later. Then, Gerald left Richmond for a faculty position at his alma mater, the University of Chicago, where he initiated its first film studies program. As one of the most innovative scholars in the field, with several significant books to his credit, he made a positive impact on the teaching of film history. Unfortunately, he passed away at 48 from AIDS, having been preceded in death by his longtime partner, who also died from AIDS. By the late 1980s, I had counted 38 friends lost to this disease.

As for my teaching schedule, I enjoyed teaching Modern British Fiction, which included the works of James Joyce, Virginia Woolf, and Joseph Conrad, as well as another course, "Great Film Directors," which in its first year featured the works of John Ford, one of Hollywood's most important directors. In the following year, I offered a course in which the entire semester was devoted to a close reading of Joyce's Ulysses. It proved to be very popular and was repeated every semester. As I related earlier, as the Vietnam War raged on, students began to devote more time to protests than their studies. The faculty was torn between their commitments to teaching and research and the socio-political interests of their students. The War substantially affected the development and growth of the college, as we had originally intended.

In the early 1980s, I was feeling uneasy about the future of the college, so I wrote an essay, not for publication, expressing regret that our academic experiment at Richmond was not developing as we had planned. Somehow, the essay reached the desk of CUNY Chancellor Joseph Murphy. He asked me to meet with him to discuss my thoughts, which, as you will later read, led to a positive change in my academic life. In 1983. Richmond College was at a decisive moment in its very young history, but the course of our future seemed to be not in the college community but in politician's hands and bad luck. Staten Island residents, as well as their political representatives, were largely conservative, their values clashing with our aspirations for the college. So, when a respected RC faculty member gave a public address on the Vietnam War to a large local audience, he was heckled, labeled a "Marxist," and vilified in the local newspaper. Faculty and students supported him, believing that academic disputes were best decided on campus by faculty, students, and administrative staff, not by politicians or the media. However, what resulted was even more powerful. The city's budget determined the fate of the college.

NEH Summer seminar

Despite this crisis, I continued teaching, published three books between 1973 and 1977, and in 1980, I was awarded a grant by the National Endowment for the Humanities (NEH) to conduct a six-week summer seminar for college professors. The subject focused on how nonfiction films could be used in humanities courses. I had not applied for this opportunity but was informed that Pauline Kael, the film critic for The New Yorker, recommended me as the leader of the group. The professors chosen for this seminar were not yet tenured and thus vulnerable to the wave of faculty firings taking place across the country due to declining enrollments in humanities courses. The staff at the NEH hoped that by introducing these vulnerable professors to the variety and quality of nonfiction films relevant to their areas of interest, they might make these courses more attractive to students. After reviewing numerous applications for this seminar, for which participants received a generous stipend to cover their living expenses in Manhattan, I selected 12 professors from across the country. Overall, they were eager to learn about the importance and usefulness of nonfiction films. We had a wonderful summer together, responded positively, and came up with fresh ideas. Several of them later reported that they had successfully integrated films into their courses, thereby increasing enrollments and preserving their jobs.

Mark Berman: Part Two

One day that summer, the seminar was interrupted by a secretary saying there was an urgent phone call for me. The Baron de Breffny, who was traveling in Spain with Mark, was calling to say that Mark had collapsed in Madrid and was in the hospital. Without further explanation, he added that he had to return to Ireland immediately and so asked if I were free to take over the situation. It was the plea of a coward, afraid of being held responsible for what had happened to Mark. I notified Mark's mother, and she flew to Madrid to accompany Mark back to New York Presbyterian Hospital (NYP). By the time Mark returned to Manhattan, he had already lost the use of his legs, and the initial diagnosis, later verified, was Multiple Sclerosis (MS), a disease for which no cure was known then and now. After a few weeks, he was moved from NYP to the Rusk Rehabilitation unit of New York University Hospital. Edgar and I prepared ourselves for the loss of our dear friend. As I have said before, his mother was a very complicated person. In particular, she resented me and my relationship with her son. She would not accept that there was no cure for MS, and thus, haunting the hospital halls, she annoyed his doctors by telling them that they should try strange remedies or procedures she had read about. In addition, she continually annoyed staff, who had to tolerate her because she was family. Edgar and I visited Mark almost daily, and when she saw us, she tried to conceal her presence by ducking into a room or just turning around and going down the hall to avoid talking with me. During all this, Mark remained cheerful, never complaining, even though he knew of his fate.

Some seven months later, in April 1981, Mark died. He was 31. The funeral was held in a funeral chapel near the Berman family home in Neponsit. It was a brief Jewish service; the casket was closed, and there was no reception afterward. Only a small number of people were present, including his father and brother, me and Edgar, and two of Mark's close friends. At the close of the service, his mother, gone mad with grief, screamed foul remarks at us as she was led out of the room. Her grief was inconsolable, and the next day, she committed suicide by hanging.

After Mark's death, I traveled to California for a much-needed getaway. I stayed with my parents, who had met Mark only once—at JFK airport while changing planes for a trip to Europe—and they remembered him fondly. Both were tender and comforting to me. After a week there, I went to Laguna Beach to stay with my friend Walter Strohm, who had never met Mark. As was his custom, we spent the morning on the beach and the afternoon by the pool at his house. Laguna is a gay haven. I didn't feel much like swimming, so I enjoyed soaking up the sun while reading a book titled Zen and the Art of Motorcycle Maintenance: An Inquiry into Values, a deceptively titled philosophical treatise that offers much to ponder. A gay man wearing a black Speedo, just like mine, stopped to comment on the title. His name is Chuck Peddie, and while he knew Walter, they clearly were not friends. Walter was a snob, and Chuck did not meet his standards.

I immediately liked him and explained the book to maintain his attention. He suggested we body-surf the waves, and afterward, he invited me for a beer. We returned to his apartment and shared much more than just beer. He was incredibly attractive. We were the same age and got along very well. Walter, who was at least twenty years older than me, was not pleased. And while Walter offered no comfort for my grief over Mark, Chuck instinctively helped me cope during those first weeks. He helped me accept that nothing could have been done to change the outcome of the disease that took Mark. Chuck was both kind and comforting. One day, he took me on his motorcycle for a long ride into the mountains. It was noisy and uncomfortable, clinging to him by the waist the whole trip, but it was enjoyable because Chuck made it so.

I returned twice to visit Chuck in Laguna. Later, after I had met Edgar, we spent a weekend at Walter's house. He invited a group of his gay friends to meet us and included Chuck at my request. Chuck eventually settled down with his partner in Palm Springs, another gay mecca. We have maintained a friendship even though for the past fifty years we haven't seen each other. But, as Tennessee Williams said, "Time doesn't take away from friendship, nor does separation."

Chapter Thirteen:
New York's Gay Life

The Gay Rights Movement

The Stonewall Uprising, which occurred on June 28, 1969, sparked the emergence of the gay liberation movement, further shaped three years later by the first fatalities of the AIDS crisis. This period brought fear, suffering, mourning, and sorrow to the gay community. Today's diverse New York gay community stands on this foundation. From this history, young people learn and remember how fragile gay rights were then and continue to be due to our nation's unpredictable politics. The uprising is now commemorated by the Stonewall National Monument and Visitor Center, located at the actual site in Greenwich Village. Too many people lived and died for the cause of homosexual freedom, making it fitting that we honor and remember them. Today's gay community is collectively referred to as LGBTQIA+, an acronym that includes a wide range of individuals, both male and female. Whether this diverse group remains united seems to depend on the who, what, where, why, and when of its continually evolving nature. Regardless of the direction it takes, it will be a vibrant mix of remarkable people. I reflect on the "golden age" based on my personal memories of experiencing it.

My Early Experiences In The Gay Community

My account begins in 1967, the year I moved to Manhattan, alone and unattached, and covers my experiences in the gay community until 1977, the year I met Edgar Munhall, who remained my partner for the next 40 years and whom you will meet in the following chapter. Being gay is a way of life, with sex at its core. Now at my age, I accept a certain truth that exemplifies the Biblical saying, "The spirit is willing, but the flesh is weak." Christ was referring to the disciples who were on the verge of temptation and ignored their duties to watch and pray. In my secular interpretation, as far as sex is concerned, the meaning for me now at 86 is impotence. I continue to have the spirit for sex and a passionate desire, yet the flesh is unable to respond. Viagra and its competitor drugs did not help me. Although many people say that I look 65, that provides little comfort. Looks don't mean much when one can no longer be enjoy having sex.

Before I moved to New York, I didn't pay much attention to the gay bars in Southern California. Sure, I had a social life, but it didn't revolve around cruising the bars. The area known as West Hollywood, home to many gay men and often referred to as "Boy's Town," was beginning to develop a gay community but hadn't yet reached its full potential. This was understandable due to laws restricting gay bars and the "not in my backyard" mentality of some residents. Unlike San Francisco, the Gay Liberation movement hadn't yet made a significant impact in making Los Angeles safe for gay individuals. It was no San Francisco. For that reason, I would venture up north to

Frisco to enjoy places like The Black Cat, Finocchio's, and The Stud. They welcomed me, and I felt like I truly belonged there.

In contrast, during my early years in Manhattan, I explored the gay bar scene in Greenwich Village, which was then known as the gay ghetto. I found the atmosphere to be nearly as liberal in its attitudes and activities as anywhere in San Francisco. A great place to begin my journey was to grab a drink at Julius's, a gay bar situated in the heart of the West Village. Young men frequented the bar, many of whom came from Ivy League schools. You would also see older businessmen, often referred to as the Brooks Brothers crowd. If you were seeking the young, hot, and flashy type of gay man, you could easily find him elsewhere in the Village. Julius primarily catered to gay, white males, and I seldom saw black, brown, or Asian faces there. While it wasn't explicitly exclusive, gaining entry was challenging if you didn't meet the doorman's approval. This scrutiny was necessary to filter out potential troublemakers who might disrupt the patrons. I found the gay bars in Harlem and Spanish Harlem to be far more welcoming than those in the Village. The doormen there simply checked your ID and sobriety level, wishing you a pleasant evening as you entered.

The Gay Liberation Movement

The Gay Liberation Movement, most active in the 1970s and 1980s, changed gay life dramatically. It garnered prime newspaper coverage that, in turn, encouraged gay people to come out to friends and family, live an openly gay life, and take direct action when necessary. With my former boyfriend, David Roggensack, I attended planning meetings of the Gay Liberation Front, founded by Arthur Bell and Arthur Evans, two of our friends. I participated in some of their demonstrations, although I didn't follow through with joining groups like Act Up, although I also knew its founder, Larry Kramer. When he was working on screenplays in London, he became friends with Bill Graf, my cousin-in-law, who was head of the office there. When Kramer returned to New York and Bill took me to meet him, I found him to be very pleasant. However, his public image was different. He was possibly by far the most public, most vocal, and most effective of the activists, as seen in his writing, particularly the Broadway play The Normal Heart. He was the founder of ACT UP (AIDS Coalition to Unleash Power), a radical group that became the loudest, most productive group devoted to the health care of people with AIDS. It influenced change not just in Washington, DC, but across the world.

The Stonewall Uprising

On June 29, 1969, I received a phone call early in the morning alerting me to a major demonstration planned for Christopher Street in Greenwich Village. The evening before, the historic Stonewall Inn had been raided and devastated by New York policemen. This demonstration was not only to protest the actions of the New York Police Department (NYPD), but also the city laws that discriminated against gays and gay bars. I attended the demonstration and witnessed gay New Yorkers who had endured violence and injury the night before. On this day, they engaged in the first significant fight for gay liberation that New Yorkers had ever witnessed. The NYPD reacted by arresting hundreds of participants in the uprising. Protests continued into the following day and throughout the first week of July. Remarkably, there were no fatalities. The achievements of this activism, broadcast around the world, have become a part of history. Gay rights organizations, conferences, and publications began to flourish. Eventually, The NYPD stopped their entrapment of individuals in gay bars, and the courts overturned existing regulations. laws that persecuted LGBTQIA+ people simply for enjoying drinks with friends. Now, the laws would protect them.

The Stonewall Inn may have been physically destroyed, but this triggered the rapid development in New York City of more than twenty-five new gay bars (e.g., The Anvil and the Mine shaft) and bathhouses (the Club Baths and Everard Baths). In these places, we could drink and cruise without fear of police harassment or arrest. Following is how I saw the gay bar scene in this new era.

New Gay bars

The liveliest bars attracted a crowd comprising everyone from everyday working New Yorkers and college students seeking new friends to those striking exaggeratedly masculine poses, relishing the attention they garnered. Indeed, your attire either granted you entry or it didn't. You needed the muscular doorkeeper's approval, who wore a stern expression while evaluating your age, appearance, physical fitness, clothing, sobriety, and, of course, the outline of your jeans, the ever-present emphasis on size. In fact, the less fabric you wore and the more you resembled a gym idol, the easier it was to be accepted. A Harley motorcycle parked outside only boosted your appeal. It's clear why the fashion world is largely run by gay men and women, as much like the fashion advertisements where models boast of their other-worldly appearance, the guys entering gay bars also sported a similarly exaggerated style. Just like trying to join an exclusive fraternity, you had to seem eager to get inside to be invited in.

The more traditional bars attracted a diverse crowd, including men from manual trades and those in financial offices, worn-out older drinkers enjoying newfound freedom, young men learning the ropes, and the jealous know-it-all types who tried to belittle you verbally. There were rough characters, both from trades and outside them; genuinely handsome men who might flirt with you, and the unfortunately unattractive ones who wished to flirt but often found themselves alone; and the occasional drag queen as well.

The toughest gay bars were often found in basements or abandoned warehouses, creating a dark, deserted, menacing, and uninviting atmosphere that many men craved. They resembled stage sets, with those who managed to get inside playing the roles of actors. These leather bars required patrons to have a specific appearance. Men who gained entry typically wore black leather jackets and pants or military surplus shirts paired with jeans. They had strong physiques, hairy chests, and bold postures. Even the bartenders were attractive. Role-playing was central to the experience. In the dark corners, unusual sexual acts pushed men's physical boundaries.

Danger lurked silently in these bars, and a hook-up between two men could lead to unpredictable consequences. This dynamic is vividly illustrated in Cruising, William Friedkin's 1980 film set in the kind of NYC gay bars just described. The movie is based on the bag murders of six gay men between 1975 and 1977, where each victim was dismembered, placed in a garbage bag, and discarded in the Hudson River. The identities of the victims have never been confirmed, but a man named Paul Bateson was convicted of one of the killings and served approximately twenty-five years in prison. My friend, journalist Arthur Bell, published a series of articles in 1979 on these unsolved murders, which sparked demands to halt the film's production. Bell argued that it unfairly portrayed gay people and could incite violence against the gay community. Al Pacino, the film's star, responded that he did not view the film as anti-gay and emphasized his desire to never harm the gay community. As a film historian, I find that this movie offers a realistic and chilling representation of the environment where the murderer found his victims. One thing is certain: this film serves as a warning for anyone who identifies as gay to exercise caution wherever they go out in the evening.

One night, two friends, who went frequently to the Mineshaft, asked me to accompany them. They dressed in full black leather, while I wore old jeans, a black tee shirt, and a leather jacket. The doorman said I could not enter because my leather jacket was brown instead of black, so I checked it with him, and he let me in. Inside, I was confronted by the super-masculine presence of a crowd that looked like a bunch of actors, all vying for the same part. Here, I saw a world of perversity I could not imagine, which included hog tying, toe sucking, piss drinking, armpit licking, dog collaring, master worshiping, fisting, and tit torturing, to name just a few. Naked men were chained to columns to allow other guys to piss on or whip them. These real activities were meant to be painful. Looks and remarks made casual observers like me out of place.

Unlike the San Francisco gay community, which endured the tragic murder of the gay politician Harvey Milk, NYC did not experience such crimes. However, newspapers occasionally reported on gruesome murders, whether solved or unsolved, involving single men who may or may not have been gay, and the culprits were rarely caught. This information resonates with the dark dangers portrayed in the Friedkin film. People in Greenwich Village faced the disruptive weekend presence of young punks from New Jersey or Queens, who drove through the Village shouting homophobic slurs at men on the sidewalks, hurling beer cans, and instigating fights with strangers. These thugs were too young to risk leaving their cars and confronting a group of angry gay men. Nonetheless, they faced arrests and served time in prison or paid fines for their actions.

Almost simultaneously, there was a significant shift in the popularity from traditional gay bars to new disco bars that welcomed a more diverse crowd, admitting not only gay men but also women and straight people eager to dance. Current fashion overshadowed the typical gay look, and drugs were rampant, particularly amphetamines, angel dust, LSD, Quaaludes, cocaine, poppers, and, of course, marijuana. The DJs, who became stars in this scene, sensed the vibe of the room and chose music accordingly, which blasted from multiple speakers until well after dawn. The most popular discos in Manhattan included The Saint (which had a predominantly White crowd), the Paradise Garage (with its majority Black crowd), the Sanctuary, the Loft, and Studio 54. The latter, which gained international fame, was housed in an old theater and was exclusive enough to attract not only Hollywood and Broadway stars but also members of international royalty. It was notoriously known for allowing open sexual activity on the balcony of the former theater. I remember going up there to watch and soon got involved myself, aware that Liza Minnelli was nearby, having her own fun. This disco scene, catering to a gay clientele while embracing some diversity, came to an end in the late 1980s. That's not to say that disco was dead, as discotheques continued into the early hours across New York City, especially in the Meatpacking District, the Lower East Side in Manhattan, and Williamsburg in Brooklyn. Although I once was a pretty good dancer and wise enough to steer clear of drugs, I am now too old to shake my booty.

I have learned a lot from visiting these bars and clubs. One idea was reaffirmed time and again: being gay is a way of life that touches all aspects of one's existence. Looking back, I was never a card-carrying member of any of the groups I've mentioned, as I was shy and tended more toward serious books and films. I longed to meet the right man but did not seek him out in gay bars or restaurants, public restrooms, or secluded areas like the Ramble in Central Park. I felt that I really didn't belong in these places. I remained close to my gay friends and mourned the loss of so many others to AIDS. In that context, the world of gay bars and clubs was not significant to me.

Age, experience, occupation, and my future expectations contributed significantly to this assumption. After all, New York City provided anything a person could desire. I was achieving meaningful academic success, forming friendships with interesting people, and adapting to the Manhattan lifestyle. Difficult experiences with Mark Berman and Jon Warner left me yearning for a lasting friendship with a New Yorker who was grounded, played by the rules and would join me in creating a happy life for both of us.

Chapter Fourteen: Edgar Munhall

I Meet My Match

On November 17, 1977, I met Edgar Munhall, not in a dark gay bar but in a gymnastics studio filled with sunlight. He was 44, and I was 39. It was my second week there and his first. The one-hour class began at 7 A.M., and we were assigned to a group of ten people, which included talented gymnasts, those who were not as talented, and beginners like us. We sat together on the floor at the edge of the room. Each one-hour class started with the instructor demonstrating a simple set of exercises, asking each of us in turn to follow his example, after which he provided his critique. In other words, we learned from him as well as from one another. Since I had done some gymnastics in college, I knew the basics, but Edgar, who had no gymnastics experience, fumbled his attempt and laughed at himself. The others took their work more seriously, but he returned to his spot next to me on the floor and kept laughing. He lacked physical experience in what was expected, even though, as he later told me, he was the national backstroke swimming champion at Yale and had been selected for the backup swimming team for the 1976 Olympics. I thought that anyone who can perform clumsily and then laugh at himself in front of others is my kind of man.

Edgar was reluctant when I asked him, more than once, to join me for coffee after our workouts. Although it was only 8:30 A.M. by the time we finished showering and dressing, he said he had to get to work and could not take the time. That was step one in my attempt to become his friend. Step two came when he told me he was the Chief Curator of The Frick Collection, and I assumed he must be a very interesting person. Step three came when, after a month of his still being too busy to have coffee before work, I looked him up in the telephone directory (remember those?), phoned him at home, and boldly said, "I want a date," to which he cordially replied with a definite sigh, "Oh, alright, come to dinner tomorrow night." That sigh said that I had finally met my match.

In Manhattan, it was unusual for someone to extend such a dinner invitation on such short notice and in their own home, but it made me feel that everything would be alright. So, the next night, I found myself in his apartment at the corner of East 55th Street and First Avenue. Before dinner, we each had a few Negronis, and before I knew it, we were in bed. The sexual experience was a perfect start to what would develop into an extraordinary relationship. Equally perfect was the dinner that followed: Osso Buco, salad, cheeses, dessert, and plenty of red wine. Edgar was a very good cook. During dinner, he explained that his initial coldness when we first met stemmed from recently ending a difficult relationship, the first serious one he'd ever had. He feared he might never find someone who could make him happy. I assured him that I would do my best to achieve that goal for both of us. Even then, I felt that he would become the most important person in my life.

Edgar was born on March 14, 1933, in Pittsburgh, as the second son of Anna Burns Munhall and Walter Munhall. Having a child during the Great Depression was a brave decision, but his parents, who already had one son, Walter, Jr., four years earlier, desired another child. His father graduated from Penn State University with a degree in hydraulic engineering but struggled to find work as the economic crisis deepened, which forced him to take a job as a painter and paper hanger. During those years, the family resided in a small house in a row of houses on a steep mountain in Pittsburgh's South Side neighborhood, one of the city's poorest areas. Their home overlooked the Jones and Laughlin Steelworks, and the noise and polluted air from the factory created an unpleasant environment for raising children. Since the steelworks operated around the clock, escaping this hazardous atmosphere was difficult. Edgar was a frail child afflicted with rheumatic fever, which sent him to the hospital more than once. In the year before I met him, he had been hospitalized again due to rheumatic fever.

By the late 1930s, when the economy had strengthened, his father was appointed the Chief Engineering Officer of the Pittsburgh Water Department, a position he would hold until retirement. This new job and salary allowed the family to move to Shadyside, a leafy neighborhood that was as different from their previous surroundings as possible. Edgar's mother, Anna, was a first-grade teacher in the Pittsburgh public schools during the early years of their marriage, but she soon retired to focus on her family. In his spare time, his father was a talented amateur photographer; after his father's death, Edgar curated an exhibition of his work at the Carnegie Museum of Art in Pittsburgh.

Academic Career

Edgar attended public schools. During his senior year at Allderdice High School, he graduated with high honors in the midterm, and the day after, he moved to New York City to study fashion drawing at the Art Students League. A few months later, Edgar's father, disapproving of fashion drawing, insisted that he apply to Yale University, where he was accepted with a full academic scholarship. After a year in an interdisciplinary honors program focusing on history, the arts, and letters, he decided to major in art history. Throughout his undergraduate years, he was a member of the men's swimming team, specializing in the backstroke, and he earned two Varsity letters as well as a national championship. At Yale, he graduated with a B.A. with High Honors in 1955 and received a Ph.D. in 1959, pausing in between to earn an M.A. in art history in 1957 from the Institute of Fine Arts at New York University. After earning his doctorate, he was appointed Assistant Professor of Art History at Yale and simultaneously served as Assistant Curator of Prints and Drawings at the Yale University Art Gallery. However, after six years in these roles, he sought a curatorial career instead of a professorial one and left New Haven for New York.

The Frick Collection

Henry Clay Frick, a Pittsburgh coke and steel magnate, assembled one of the world's greatest art collections, originally displayed for family and guests in his mansion on New York's Fifth Avenue. The art collection, regarded as one of the finest in the world, includes old master paintings, Renaissance bronzes, French clocks, porcelains, sculptures, and furniture. His will specified that, upon his death, the mansion would be transformed into a public museum as a gift to the citizens of New York City, which finally occurred in 1935. The curatorial responsibilities were managed by the director and Frick's daughter, Helen. However, a public museum of such significance needed a professional staff, so in 1965, at age 32, Edgar was hired as its first Curator.

In this role, Edgar led the transformation of a domestic mansion into a modern public museum. Learning from some of the world's great house museums, he created the framework for such a museum, establishing the necessary departments and hiring the best people to work in them. He supervised acquisitions, gallery installations, publications, art conservation, and lectures, and he originated the museum's exhibition program and organized many innovative exhibitions himself.

Through his acquisitions on behalf of the museum, Edgar enriched the collection with paintings by Bruegel the Elder, Ingres, Liotard, Memling, Raeburn, and Watteau; drawings by Boucher, and Corot. Claude Lorrain, Greuze, and Ingres; prints by Van Dyck and

Whistler; sculptures by Algardi, Bernini, and Coysevox, as well as examples of the decorative arts by the Sèvres Manufactory, and the breathtaking collection of clocks and watches bequeathed to the Frick in Edgar's honor by Winthrop K. Edey.

Edgar's scholarly achievements were extensive. His numerous articles appeared in major academic journals, and with an engaging style that garnered him a large, loyal audience, he delivered more than fifty public lectures at a variety of American and European institutions. He also organized, or co-organized, around 30 exhibitions, both large and small, many of which debuted at the Frick and later in museums across the U.S. and Europe. Post-doctoral students served as lecturers, and he mentored them as they progressed to positions as college professors, museum curators, and directors. After his retirement, he continued to serve as an art advisor to museums and private collectors.

While interested in all forms of art, both ancient and contemporary, his specialty was the 18th-century French artist Jean-Baptiste Greuze (1725-1805). In 1976, he organized the first exhibition dedicated to Greuze, which was displayed at the Wadsworth Atheneum in Hartford, the California Palace of the Legion of Honor in San Francisco, and the Musée des Beaux-Arts in Dijon, France. His final exhibition, Greuze the Draftsman, was presented in 2002 at the Frick Collection and the J. Paul Getty Museum in Los Angeles. It was praised by art critic John Russell in the New York Times as "a majestic achievement." Edgar gained international acclaim as the leading expert on Greuze's art. In recognition of Edgar's contribution to the promotion of French culture, the French government named him Chevalier in the Ordre des Arts et des Lettres in 1989, later promoting him to Officier in 2002.

Edgar and I made some good friends among the Frick Staff. Among them are Manu von Miller and Amy Herman. Manu, who has Austrian roots, was a protégée of Edgar's and became a good friend. She and her husband, Markus, now live in Munich, where she is an independent art historian and art researcher. She is also a passionate music lover, lucky to be able to attend concerts in Vienna and Berlin, as well as the summer festivals in Salzburg and Bayreuth. In the past few years after Edgar's death, the three of us have enjoyed opera in Munich and the Berlin Philharmonic Orchestra in its hometown. They also visit the U.S.A. to see friends, attend concerts, and enjoy mountain climbing. Manu, who was very close to Edgar and me and whom we regarded as a sister, never forgets a birthday or other significant dates. I am honored to be her friend and only wish we lived closer together.

I first met Amy Herman when she was the assistant to Charles Ryskamp, then the Frick Director. A creative and ambitious individual, she established the first education program at the Frick, aimed at enriching the museum experience for every visitor, including children. She then moved on to the New York PBS station, where she developed their inaugural education program. After earning a law degree and a graduate degree in art history, she created the "Art of Perception" seminar for medical students, designed to enhance their observation, analysis, and communication skills. She believed that teaching people to observe paintings, sculptures, and photographs closely can help sharpen their visual intelligence. This led to the publication of her first book, The Art of Perception: Sharpen Your Perception, Change Your Life. Soon, she was addressing a diverse array of executives and personnel from corporations, the military, and agencies within the criminal justice system. She travels extensively, lecturing both domestically and in numerous foreign countries, and authored two additional books: Fixed: How to Perfect the Fine Art of Problem Solving and smART: Use Your Eyes to Boost Your Brain.

By sheer coincidence, Amy moved to an apartment house across the street from mine. I thought I would get to see more of her, and while it's difficult to get her to slow down and have dinner with me, we manage every few months to spend some time together. Amy has a sparkling personality, perfect for talking to different audiences, and a wicked sense of humor, perfect for talking with me. She exudes charm, intelligence, and genuine kindness, and despite these responsibilities, she has also had the time, as a single mother, to raise her son Ian.

Our Life Together

Edgar and I shared many friends in our respective professional lives and enjoyed a vibrant social life together. These friends formed two groups: those who were always part of our world and those we knew professionally but not typically in social settings. The list of the first group is lengthy. Among them, I remember most Terry Stevenson, a brilliant photographer, and Bob Allen, a glamorous art expert and bon vivant. We gathered at least twice a month with them and their partners. The delightfully eccentric clock collector Kelly Edey often joined us, along with Robert Isaacson, an art dealer, and Matthew Benedict, a talented young artist whose career Edgar was helping to guide. Other close friends included Tony Bocchi, a film expert; Guy Bauman, a curator at the Metropolitan Museum; and his partner, Duncan Stalker, an editor at Vanity Fair.

Of all these friends, Tony is the one I have known the longest. He was born and raised in Brazil but moved to this country in his twenties. Eventually, he became a U.S. citizen. He possesses expert and self-taught knowledge of world history and film history. Tony worked for many years as a butler for a prominent man who lived alone on the Upper East Side. During this time, he became acquainted with Ross Kirk, and after his employer's death, they moved to Waterbury, Connecticut. Ross, his life partner and later officially his husband, lost his eyesight and relies not only on Tony but also on a seeing-eye dog. Although Ross has mastered all the computer programs that help him work as if he were not blind, Tony takes great care of him. Ross, who swims daily at the YMCA, leads an active life. Tony and I maintain contact through the internet but seldom spend time together. He has many talents and virtues, especially loyalty.

We were fortunate to have a circle of friends who belonged to what was then referred to as high society, a world that enjoyed a prosperous relationship with the art world, and in his role, Edgar thrived in both. However, whenever he was invited to their parties or dinners, he politely reminded them that he did not travel alone and requested that they include me on the guest list. Although this was an unusual request, his wish was granted. Before long, as a couple, we were going out several nights a week, often in black tie, to be welcomed by some of New York's most notable hosts and hostesses, including Brooke Astor and Charles and Jayne Wrightsman.

While in college, fueled by his enthusiasm for everything French, Edgar spent his summers in France, getting to know the great restaurants and using his access to the Louvre as a base from which to visit Europe's other renowned museums. His connections in the French art and social circles were as one might expect, and behind them was his close friend and social mentor, Madame Berthe David-Weill, the wife of one of France's most prominent bankers, a woman he often referred to as "the uncrowned Queen of France." In the following years, we enjoyed old-world hospitality at her Fifth Avenue apartment, houses in Paris, and an apartment in Venice. Her chef, butler, and other staff were exceptional. She frequently entertained, rotating a series of guests so that there was always someone new, like Rudolf Nureyev, then the most famous male dancer in the world, who unexpectedly arrived late one day for lunch, wearing his rehearsal clothes, and effortlessly charmed everyone. Berthe was captivated by him, even though it was their first meeting. She seated him to her right, and during their conversation, which everyone strained to hear, she asked him for the name of the male dancer's undergarment. He replied, "jock strap," but since he spoke softly and she was nearly deaf, she didn't understand. Therefore, she turned to Edgar on her left and asked him to repeat it. She repeated "jock strap" so loudly that the people at the table erupted into laughter.

Berthe was also very kind to me. She had a passion for movies, and listened to them by reading the lips of actors. Indeed, she could read lips in four languages. She enjoyed going to the movies in the afternoon and often asked me to accompany her and explain anything in the film she didn't understand. Afterward, we treated ourselves to hot chocolate and pastries at Rumpelmayers on Central Park South. Typically, she preferred restaurants she knew well and was cautious about those she hadn't tried. With a personal chef who was undoubtedly the best French cook in New York, it was challenging to invite her over for our home-cooked meals, so we consulted with her beforehand to plan a menu she would enjoy. No to pasta of any kind; yes to steak. When she was home in Paris, she provided her friends with the full experience of her life there, including lunches and dinners that Marcel Proust would have gladly enjoyed as well.

We were also longtime friends of Baron Elie and Baroness Liliane de Rothschild, who had homes in Paris and the countryside. While the Paris house was impressive, their art collection was even more remarkable. The meals there were superb as well. Baron Elie, a sportsman, not only enjoyed being the host but also shared the funniest and dirtiest jokes one could ever hear. In contrast, Liliane was well-versed in the discussions and talents of the Parisian art and fashion worlds. Karl Lagerfeld not only designed her clothes but also harbored a crush on her, as evidenced by the two dozen red roses he had delivered to her every day she was in town. We were invited to a party to celebrate her birthday, and we made a trip to France just for that occasion. The party took place at their chateau in Chantilly, and because I was no longer driving a car, she simply called her good friend Hubert de Givenchy and asked him to take us in his car. Before we left, he showed us his house and art collection and then drove us there and back.

Although high society has played a role in our life together, it was our close friends in New York—who were our age and shared common interests—that filled the majority of our social life. We often entertained them at our respective apartments. Those meeting us for the first time were surprised to discover that we never lived together. One night at dinner in Edgar's, a guest, realizing the benefits of this arrangement, said across the table to her husband, "Robert, why didn't you think of that?" We had seriously considered living together, but since we both needed a quiet place to write, separate apartments were the solution, provided we had dinner and spent our evenings together every night. Bunny Mellon—who, along with her husband Paul, had a relationship like ours—wrote, "We lived apart so that we could be together," reflecting her experience and wisdom, as well as our preference. When traveling, of course, Edgar and I happily shared hotel rooms.

Aaron Copland became a good friend after we met him through Sophronus Mundy, an old pal of Edgar's who looked after the composer at his upstate retreat, Rock Hill, in Cortlandt Manor. At that time, Copland was in his 80s and showing the first signs of Alzheimer's disease. Although he rarely left home, he ventured into

Manhattan to take us to Carnegie Hall to hear composer Virgil Thomson's Mother of Us All, a two-act opera featuring a pro-feminist libretto by Gertrude Stein. He enjoyed having guests, especially people from fields outside of music. Edgar discussed art in general and the Frick Collection in particular with him. He and I talked about his musical scores for films, including Lewis Milestone's The North Star (1943), The Red Pony (1949), and William Wyler's The Heiress (1949). He especially appreciated younger men, including our friends Guy Bauman and Duncan Stalker. Like many young people in my time, I had piano training, and when I mentioned to Aaron that I was struggling with a simple Bach prelude, he chuckled: "No truck with the moderns, eh?" with a heavy emphasis on the word moderns.

After Copland's death, and as specified in his will, his large property was transformed into an informal retreat for composers seeking a quiet place to work. The cabins featured a piano, a bathroom, and a small kitchen for their use. When he mentioned that he hoped to replace the piano in the guest house where we were staying, I gladly donated my Baldwin baby grand to him since I no longer played it.

Both Edgar and Andy Warhol, born five years apart in Pittsburgh, were destined for the art world. As children, they were invited to become members of the Tam-o-Shanters, founded by the Carnegie Museum for young people who had displayed artistic talent based on their drawings. Sharing Saturday morning classes, Edgar and Andy became friends and later continued that relationship in New York. Andy invited us to visit The Factory, the studio where he and his team created lithographs and silkscreens. Edgar responded by giving Andy a tour of the Frick Collection. I first met Warhol in a Spanish restaurant in the Village. He usually had a camera with him and took candid photos of people. Upon recognizing Edgar, he photographed us and later joined us at our table. Andy also gave us a tour of his East Side townhouse, which housed an eclectic collection later sold at auction. The Andy Warhol Museum in Pittsburgh boasts his paintings, drawings, prints, photographs, films, and videotaped works, enough to fill seven floors.

Other notable figures included some who became friends, others who were mere acquaintances, and still others we met just once. They represent a cross-section of Manhattan's art world and nightlife, but all have faded into memory. These include Dorothy Dean, an African American graduate of Radcliffe and Harvard, who was a writer and actress closely linked to the Warhol studio and its circle. She did editorial work for The New Yorker and served as the door person and bouncer at Max's Kansas City, a restaurant and nightclub that was a popular spot for the art community in the 1960s. If Dorothy let you in, you were among the chosen. Unpredictable and talented, she tragically passed away too young from cancer at 55.

Edward Gorey, the writer and illustrator of unique and enchanting books, invited me to the New York City Ballet without Edgar, after which he suggested introducing me to his torture chamber. I declined. We enjoyed several pleasant evenings with Robert Mapplethorpe in his loft. The photographer, known for his portraits of male nudes that earned him a notorious reputation, was nonetheless one of the great photographers in contemporary art history. On an entirely different level was Sir John Pope-Hennessy, the British art historian who had mentored Edgar while teaching at Yale. When I met him, he was the head of the European Paintings department at the Met Museum. He employed Sophronus Mundy, formerly Aaron Copland's caregiver, as his chef. One evening before dinner, he pointed out his new dining room chairs. One of the guests remarked that sitting on them for even a few minutes felt like torture, to which he responded in his royal manner, "I don't think dining room chairs should be comfortable, do you?"

We met Irving Penn, the distinguished photographer, and his wife, the model Lisa Fonssagrives, at a dinner at the New York apartment of the Otto and Micheline Fried. Penn pushed the boundaries of conventional photography and, for a variety of subjects, was impressive. He talked at length about this, and although it was the only time we saw them, it was unforgettable. The Frieds were based in Paris: Otto was an artist, and Micheline, a relative of Berthe David-Weill, was active in the fashion world. Back in New York, in 1988, Sissie Cahan, one of Bobby Short's closest friends, gave a party to celebrate the publication of my new book, The Vision of Robert: The Artist as Myth and Filmmaker, a study of the first American documentary filmmaker. She invited a list of our friends and hers, including the filmmakers Ismail Merchant and James Ivory, who were her neighbors and whom she thought I would enjoy meeting. The book's cover is a photograph by Richard Avedon, whom she also invited. I wanted it for the book's cover but feared his fee would be far more than my publisher, a university press, could afford. So, I phoned Avedon's office and asked if I could discuss this with him. They said that I should come right away because he wasn't busy. He offered to let me use the photograph without any charge on the condition that I give him a copy of the book. As soon as the book was printed, I delivered a signed copy to his office.

The Abdy family were prominent art dealers in London, specializing in French art. Early in his career at the Frick, Edgar met Sir Robert Abdy and his wife, Lady Jane. He and Sir Robert became close friends, and he was invited several times to their country house, called Balls, named after the two spheres that topped the entrance gates. Later, Edgar formed a friendship with their son, Sir Valentine Abdy, and his wife, Lady Mathilde. When we were in London, they invited us to lunch to meet their esteemed guest, Sir Cecil Beaton, who wore red satin pajamas and talked endlessly about himself. He is nonetheless very famous for his diverse photographic work. He also excelled in interior design and costume design for stage and screen, notably in My Fair Lady. On another trip, we spent the day at Balls with the younger Abdys, only to discover that they had redecorated the country house drawing room in striking psychedelic patterns and colors.

On our first trip to Scotland together, Edgar arranged for us to see Greuze drawings owned by the Duke and Duchess of Buccleuch, who welcomed us warmly to Bowhill House, a family residence. Their hospitality was gracious, considering that recently, there had been a theft of a Leonardo da Vinci masterpiece from their

Drumlanrig Castle nearby. It has since been returned to the family and is once again on display. I'll never forget visiting the Duke, one of Scotland's richest men, dressed in hunting attire, in the office in which he managed the affairs of his vast estates. On a trip to Ireland, we met Desmond Fitzgerald, the Knight of Glin, a lesser but equally charming royal with a hereditary Irish title. An old friend of Edgar's, he welcomed us to his castle, part of which served as a guesthouse for tourists. He was a wonderfully silly character who offered to share our bed. We avoided that but still enjoyed an excellent dinner with him and his wife.

At the Frick, where he gave a lecture, we met Colm Toíbín, the Irish writer, who flattered us extravagantly by saying we were the most sophisticated people he had met during his time in Manhattan. Another memorable morning occurred in the lobby of the Imperial Hotel in Vienna, we encountered former President Bill Clinton, who, alongside actor Sean Penn, had just represented the U.S. at an annual AIDS conference. He was checking out of the hotel, but we chatted briefly with him. As the men were about to leave, the hotel staff formed a long line, and the former President expressed gratitude to the group for their service, shook hands, and patiently spoke with each one of them before they left for their flight home.

Our Different Apartments

Edgar had just one apartment throughout his years in Manhattan. What follows is an account of where I lived in contrast to him. New Yorkers are very aware of the exact locations where people reside in

Manhattan—the neighborhood, the street, the building. It defines you more than you might initially realize. I felt at ease in the neighborhood and apartment building where I first lived. The building was located at 231 East 76th Street, nestled between 2nd and 3rd Avenues, directly across from Robert Wagner Junior High School, a three-story structure that occupies nearly the entire block. Coincidentally, Edgar and I both had our first apartments on this same block, but his residence was temporary as he awaited a move further downtown. If we ever crossed paths on that street, neither of us remembers it. My apartment was a ground-floor, one-bedroom unit in a twelve-story building, and I lived there comfortably for three decades. In 1997, seeking some change and knowing I could afford it, I relocated to the Barclay, a Glenwood corporation building with around 500 units, situated on York Avenue between 91st and 92nd Streets, overlooking the Triborough Bridge (now named for Robert F. Kennedy) and the Hell's Gate area of the East River. There, my two-bedroom, two-bath apartment was on the corner of the 32nd floor, providing a truly panoramic view that included seven major bridges. I chose it not for the neighborhood but for Asphalt Green, a public athletic complex directly across the street. I had been swimming in its Olympic-sized pool for the past year, and of all the city pools I had used, this was the best and well worth the move.

However, after ten years there, I grew tired of being in such a quiet, isolated, and sleepy neighborhood where I had to walk two or three blocks to find a coffee shop or a dry-cleaning store. So, in 2007, I moved to another Glenwood building, the Marlowe, on 81st Street, at the corner of Lexington Avenue. This lively neighborhood is just a few minutes' walk from the Metropolitan Museum and Central Park, featuring markets, restaurants, and coffee shops that make it interesting. I still took the bus to Asphalt Green for swimming. The Marlowe is a small, dignified building with fifteen floors and about eighty apartments. Mine was on the 7th floor with a direct view across 81st Street to the large house then owned by Madonna. I met her only once, in the local barbershop where she had brought her young son for a haircut. Since she was offstage and out of costume, I didn't recognize her until she asked me if I lived in the neighborhood. "Yes, I live directly across from your house," I replied. We talked about the boy she had adopted in Malawi, who was just getting familiar with living in New York. Her house attracted many foreign tourists 24 hours a day, snapping pictures and trying to see behind the high steel fence that bordered its property.

I remained at the Marlowe for ten happy years, still rotating evenings with Edgar, following the same dinner schedule: one night at my place and the next at his. By then, we had both retired, free to travel whenever and wherever we wanted while still enjoying our social life at home. As for our work, I was busy writing the sixth edition of my textbook, and Edgar continued to visit the Frick at least twice a week, where he maintained a small library carrel as his office. However, I could see that while he remained his old charming and active self, his health was declining. To me, his condition seemed quite normal for a man in his eighties; I didn't think much of it. He took taxis rather than the bus to get to and from my place. The dinners he served were far less ambitious than they once had been, but that's completely understandable when I reflect on the stylish menus we created.

It was then that he asked me to move so we could be closer to each other. In 2016, I relocated to his neighborhood and leased an apartment at the Bristol, a Glenwood building surrounded by spacious gardens on 56th Street between 2nd and 1st Avenues, just a block from Edgar's place. The Bristol, standing 33 stories tall, offers 375 apartments, and I rented a one-bedroom, one-bath unit on the 3rd floor overlooking the lush garden. The view was lovely, but the apartment was too small for the office space I needed. However, being able to walk to Edgar's apartment with only one street to cross and for him to come to mine made it the right choice. After I had been at the Bristol for three years, the Covid crisis caused many tenants to leave, resulting in numerous available units. So, I rented a two-bedroom, two-bath apartment on the 19th floor, offering a grand view of Midtown Manhattan and its towering office buildings. I turned the smaller of the two bedrooms into my office, and I am typing this from here now.

As I was preoccupied with getting settled and finishing my book, Edgar hadn't mentioned that he was seeing Dr. Jeffrey Fisher, who had been our primary care physician for many years. So I was surprised when, on Monday, October 10, 2016, he asked me to get a cab and accompany him to Dr. Fisher's office. Jeff broke an uneasy silence by telling me that he had been treating Edgar for pancreatic cancer and then delivered the even more devastating news that Edgar had less than a week to live. When I asked Edgar why he hadn't informed me earlier, he replied, as partners often do, that he didn't want to upset me. That afternoon, he was transferred to the hospice center at New York Presbyterian Hospital, and seven days later, during which I stayed with him each day, he passed away on Monday, October 17, at the age of 83.

Edgar specified in his will that he did not want a funeral or memorial service; however, if one were to occur, it should be a joyous occasion. With that in mind, I began making plans for the event to be held in November at The Frick Collection. In this effort, I received gracious and generous support from Ian Wardropper, the Frick's Director, as well as many other Frick employees. After the invitations were sent out and the responses came in, we realized the event was going to be twice as large as anticipated. Therefore, at 5:30 on Monday, November 5, approximately 250 people were seated in the East Gallery, the maximum allowed by fire laws, where the program took place. An additional 200 people crowded into every available space in the galleries and hallways, where large television screens had been set up so they could see and hear the proceedings.

The program began with the opening music of Bach's Goldberg Variations, performed by Glenn Gould, one of our favorite recordings. The speakers included the Frick's current Director, the Director Emerita, the President Emerita of the Board of Trustees, and four art historians who were either current or former staff members during Edgar's time as Chief Curator. Each was asked to keep their remarks to six minutes and to keep them light, even humorous.

Everything went smoothly. I concluded the proceedings with a brief overview of some highlights from the years Edgar and I spent together. He had a wonderful sense of humor, and I hoped my final remarks would leave his friends and colleagues laughing. And they did.

Then, with Louis Armstrong's recording of "When the Saints Go Marching In," the guests made their way into the flower-filled garden court for champagne and hors d'oeuvres, sharing their stories and memories of Edgar. Now, eight years later, people still stop me on the street to tell me how much they liked Edgar and that they will always remember the memorial service.

Chapter Fifteen:
People And Places

Prominent People I Have Met

Throughout my lifetime, I have encountered many prominent individuals. Let's begin with the world of film: Lillian Gish, a remarkable star from both silent and sound eras; Francis Ford Coppola, the director best known for The Godfather; George Cukor, the Hollywood director renowned for his work with leading ladies; Judy Garland, one of those stars; Harry Carey, Jr., an early film actor and a friend of my father's; Julie Christie, a British actress who gave me slices of her apple while we watched a movie at the Telluride Film Festival; Gloria Swanson, acclaimed as the most beloved silent film actress of all time and who regained fame in 1950 as the star of Sunset Boulevard; Montgomery Clift, whom I assisted in walking to his Manhattan home when he was too intoxicated to make it on his own; and Myrna Loy, one of my favorites, who was shopping and, out of the blue, asked me to recommend a good brand of pasta. In the same store, I was literally confronted by Elaine Stritch, who was, as we politely say, three sheets to the wind and who pushed me aside and hurled some unprintable insults at me.

Other unforgettable people I've met include Marilyn Monroe, Jacqueline Kennedy Onassis, Leni Riefenstahl, Mick Jagger, Greta Garbo, Marlene Dietrich, Sean Connery, Jan Morris, and Ann

Patchett. I met Marilyn Monroe in Hollywood on a sweltering night as she stepped out of her white limousine to attend a performance by Yves Montand. A large crowd applauded her arrival, but since I stood at the curb next to her car, she took my hand to help her exit gracefully. Dressed in a long, fitted gown, she needed assistance. As she got out of the car, she brushed a few strands of hair aside and whispered to me, "Warm," in her signature breathless voice. You might wonder how I found myself in this situation, and the simple answer is that I had a ticket to the show and had been informed by someone in the crowd that she was attending that night. Since she took my hand and whispered to me, I can proudly claim that we met.

Jacqueline Kennedy Onassis could often be seen strolling in Central Park, where my dog Dylan and I had the great pleasure of meeting and talking to her. It was fall, and she wore a long coat of deep green. Dylan, a Jack Russell terrier full of vitality and, encouraged by her, jumped into her arms. He acted like the gentleman he was, resting in her arms while she and I discussed the dogs we had owned over the years. I apologized for any dirt the dog might have left on her coat, but she graciously waved that off and praised his good behavior. Although she had an appointment and needed to leave, she expressed hope that we might meet again in the park; alas, we never did.

Leni Riefenstahl, born in Berlin in 1902, was an actress before becoming a producer and director during the years surrounding Adolf Hitler's rise to power. Although she was cleared of being a member of the Nazi Party, she faced international scorn throughout her life for her film work with the Reich. As a historian of documentary film, I knew her film "Triumph of the Will," which is said to be an account of the 1934 Nazi Party rally that drew around 700,000 attendees but is a propaganda film that supports Hitler. It holds major significance in the history of political films. After signing a contract with Indiana University Press to write a book about it for their series of short film guides, I first wanted to meet the woman behind it. I obtained a research grant and flew to Munich, where I spent two weeks with her, going to her studio daily to review materials in her meticulous archive, stored in a vault worthy of any bank. Her archivist was a small, elderly woman, and I was amazed by her neatness and organizational skills. Mark Berman accompanied me as my assistant, and Leni developed a fondness for him, insisting he sit beside her and hold her hand. She was gracious and accommodating, allowing me to tape several hours of her comments. She also granted me permission to write her biography, but after my film guide was published, she remarked that while I had done a good job, she would write her own life story. Numerous so-called biographies about her exist, most of which are worthless. Her autobiography, simply titled "Memoir," received critical acclaim; the New York Times named it one of the notable books of 1995. However, Leni had a poor memory of facts and showed no hesitation in telling lies or distorting information regarding her years in the Third Reich. Her historical accounts are not reliable.

She never stopped working, skin diving, and skiing at an advanced age, spending many of her remaining years in Africa while photographing people from tribes that were nearly forgotten. Much later, when the Telluride Film Festival honored her (along with Gloria Swanson and Francis Ford Coppola) with lifetime achievement awards, she accepted and asked me to accompany her to Colorado as her companion. The film crowd, including many critics and historians, was eager to meet her, and she obliged many of them. However, these greetings ceased when several hundred members of the Denver Jewish community arrived to protest her work for the Reich. They marched up and down the streets, and when she attempted to speak to the crowd, many spat at her and, unfortunately, at me as well.

I met Mick Jagger twice. The first time was backstage at a Rolling Stones concert in New York City. While preparing my history of the nonfiction film, I wrote a section on the films of the Maysles Brothers, including Gimme Shelter (1970), which focuses on the Rolling Stones in the USA. Albert Maysles, grateful for my attention, invited me to a Stones concert where they would be shooting some footage for that film. As I waited to see the show from backstage, I was surprised to see Jagger vomit just before going onstage, later learning that many nervous performers do that. It's hard to imagine Jagger being nervous, but I found him to be a very shy, gentle man when Maysles introduced me to him in the backstage green room. Mick pulled me aside and asked numerous questions about my work on nonfiction films. Our second meeting was arranged by Peter Beard, the American photographer who spent much of his career documenting people and animals in Africa. Edgar knew him from

Yale, and I knew him from his books, which are gems in their field. Out of the blue, he called me to say that Mick wanted to meet Riefenstahl and asked if I could help arrange it. As it happened, she was soon coming to New York for a meeting with her publisher, so I set up a meeting. Mick and his first wife Bianca were staying at the Plaza, so we started there. First, I introduced them to Leni. She already knew Peter Beard through their shared interest in photographing African tribes. After the two of us were seated in the suite, originally Frank Lloyd Wright's New York studio, a door opened at the far end of the long room, and Mick did his famous strut toward me, chanting in his signature accent, "Richud, Richud," as a way of thanking me for arranging the meeting. He had carefully planned our day. First, Mick took us in a limo to a fish restaurant for lunch; then, we boarded a helicopter to take us out to Beard's house in Montauk. After a tour, we had tea, leaving Mick and Leni alone to walk and talk on the cliff high above the beach. She remembered him telling her that he had screened Triumph of the Will several times, mesmerized by Hitler's tactics for holding a huge crowd's attention. There was nothing that he did not know about mesmerizing crowds! Then, alas, it was time for the helicopter to return us to Manhattan.

In the early 1970s, during the Christmas season, I visited Cartier's hoping to find something nice for a low price, as they had a small boutique dedicated to that purpose. Completely engrossed in examining the $25 gifts, I didn't notice the other shoppers until I heard the distinctive voice of Marlene Dietrich speaking to me: "Young man, if you were to choose a gift for your doctor, which of these thermometers would you select, the silver or the gold?" It was her! Lacking experience in selecting gifts for doctors, I replied: "I think the gold one might be too extravagant and could send the wrong message to other patients, so perhaps the silver one?" After asking the salesperson to charge and wrap it, she invited me to share coffee and pastries with her in a nearby private room that Cartier reserved for individuals like her (and me). I mentioned that my friend Charles Silver, the head of MOMA's film studies department, had just published a new book about her, which she expressed interest in reading. However, instead of discussing movies, we talked about life in general. She was interested in my background, my writing about film, why I lived in New York instead of Los Angeles, and my future. It was a delightful hour during which we must have enjoyed three espressos each and Cartier's delicious Christmas cookies before parting ways. As soon as I returned home, I called Charles Silver and said, "You wouldn't believe who I just met!"

Although we often see celebrities on the streets of New York, there is a shared understanding that we should treat them as ordinary citizens and avoid staring, asking for autographs, or fawning over them. They have earned their privacy, and the cool thing is to act as if we don't see them. So, while I was on Second Avenue in the 70s, near where I lived, I tried to be a good citizen when I saw Greta Garbo standing next to me, waiting for the traffic light to change. However, I couldn't help myself and turned to look at her, dressed in men's clothes: a baseball cap, dark glasses, a plaid shirt, Levis, and sneakers. When she noticed me staring, she playfully ducked behind a large mailbox. She poked her head around and smiled, suggesting she wanted to play a sort of game of hide-and-seek, so we did that for a few minutes before we exchanged hellos. Her laughter and sense of play showed me that she wasn't the ice goddess of legend. She asked if I had time to walk with her to Bobby Dazzler, a men's store a block away. I had plenty of time. Although I knew the two guys who owned the store, I realized that she wanted to be alone to shop in peace.

If it seems that the only notable people I run into or meet are women, that's not the case. Bobby Short's agent invited a stellar crowd to a cocktail party celebrating his years in show business. While Bobby and I arrived and left together, he spent the rest of the time working the room. I watched as Lauren Bacall made a star's entrance as she arrived with Sean Connery. Although she was with Connery, she engaged with the other guests and left him on his own. He stood for a while all by himself as if nobody recognized him. Recently, Pierre Chardin opened a men's boutique with some terrific clothes. I splurged and bought his famous double-breasted blue wool blazer with brass buttons, which I wore that night, along with a white wool turtleneck sweater, gray flannel trousers, and black loafers. Looking across the room, I saw Connery beckoning me to join him. He was dressed in an outfit identical to mine. He shook my hand and said, "We can't stay here. It's like two women wearing the same hat. Let's go to a bar and have a real drink." I passed by Bobby and told him what was happening and that I would return soon. We went to the nearest neighborhood spot, the Mayfair, a famous gay bar. We had a drink and received several snide remarks from patrons about our dressing like twins, but when he was recognized, they left us alone. Soon, we returned to the party in our matching outfits.

Charles Pierce was more than a friend; he was a phenomenon, a comedian who was also one of the world's leading female impersonators. To those unfamiliar with his performances in nightclubs in San Francisco, Los Angeles, and New York City, he was not what is typically identified as a drag queen. If you saw his act even once, you would never forget it. He characterized an impersonator as a type of comedian who could portray Bette Davis by adopting her look and mannerisms and then finding ways to poke fun at her, sometimes wicked but rarely cruel. His most unforgettable targets included Mae West, Joan Crawford, Gloria Swanson, Carol Channing, Shelley Winters, Tallulah Bankhead, Joan Collins, and Katharine Hepburn. Each of these women had a distinctive, unique identity on stage or screen that was ripe for parody, and Charles perfectly captured each one. It was not only his mastery of their voices but also the way they dressed and moved. Anyone who has ever witnessed Charles's Mae West will never forget it.. That she was a caricature to begin with only makes his depiction of her even more imaginative. He did not impersonate men in his act. This is a unique art form that has become somewhat dated because the current generation is largely unfamiliar with the great movie actresses of the past. Today, movie and television actresses aim to be glamorous from head to toe. I can't think of one that Charles would choose to impersonate.

Charles and I first met at Chez Freddy, a bar with a small auditorium on East 49th Street. Edgar and I were sitting at a table very close to the platform that served as the stage. I am bald, and Charles targeted me with, "I see that Gandhi has just entered the room — late!" It drew more laughs than it deserved. During his act, he revealed that his mother had recently passed away. After the show, I went backstage to express my condolences and mentioned that my mother had also died recently. He asked for my address so he could write to me, which started an overwhelming flood of mail. Sometimes, I would find three envelopes in my mailbox at once, each one funnier than the last. He sent snippets from some of his monologues, little drawings of his female subjects, and more. He also had a collection of custom-made rubber ink stamps that he frequently used to decorate the envelopes. I couldn't reply to all this correspondence, but I tried to write two or three times a week. In that one year, he sent 400 letters. Simultaneously, he was diagnosed with prostate cancer and, after an unsuccessful operation, learned he had only a short time to live. He called me to ask where he might donate his scripts, letters, photographs, and the history of his performances. I recommended the New York Public Library for the Performing Arts, and they were happy to receive the many boxes he sent. I also contributed the letters he'd sent to me. Charles lived in North Hollywood, and Edgar and I went out to spend a day with him. While he was as funny as ever, it was evident that he was very sick. Charles died in 1991, at the age of 72. A week before his death, he called to tell me that Bea Arthur would deliver the eulogy and that she wanted a joke for its conclusion, asking me to supply one. I called around, and finally, my niece spoke to the gay guys in her office, who found a joke that brought down the house. Unfortunately, I was unable to attend, but the service was filmed, and I received the tape. He was a unique actor and a good friend, and his memory lives on in my heart.

Over the years, I have developed a deep admiration for the works of British writer Jan Morris. She authored more than a hundred books. Known for her writing about the world, especially life in cities, she is often labeled a travel writer. However, her books feature sharp observations and profound reflections that align more with a philosophy of life than simply informing readers where to find a good meal. At 93, she lived in a Welsh farmhouse that she had shared with her wife for many years. In 2019, I had planned a trip to Wales and hoped to meet her, so I wrote her a letter mentioning our shared connections, including the same publisher, and invited her to join me for lunch or tea at the Portmeirion Hotel. Honoring her age and privacy, I explained to her that I was not a journalist and wouldn't interview her or publish an account of our meeting. She replied, "Mr. Barsam! Many thanks for your very kind letter – marvelous for my morale!" Several weeks later, she wrote again to confirm her availability on May 29 and that she would meet me at the hotel for breakfast at "11-ish." Although it was a cold, rainy morning, she drove herself to the hotel in an old Honda that showed signs of wear from her self-acknowledged reckless driving. As a member of the hotel's Board of Directors, she requested that they prepare breakfast and serve it in a small private dining room. Before entering, she invited me to sit in her car for a few minutes "to get acquainted." We hit it off immediately and then went inside. She was dressed in a heavy sweater, corduroy jeans, and a striking Navajo necklace made of silver and turquoise. As we entered the hotel, Fiona Peel, my friend and driver, was waiting to meet her. They shared much in common, particularly their interest in Welsh history.

Breakfast featured eggs Benedict and delicious pastries. We discussed my trip to Wales, her life in the farmhouse and the surrounding areas, and her lifelong pursuit of human kindness, which she has often written about. When it was time for her to drive back home, we said our farewells, and she gave me a gentle kiss on the lips. Then, she held my hand and gazed out at the sea before saying, "Go away, get inside, and don't watch my driving." And then she was gone, kindness personified.

Another special person who embodies kindness is Ann Patchett, the novelist, bookstore owner, and a true angel to underprivileged children for providing them with books they could not otherwise afford. When I first heard about this, I felt compelled to support her efforts to promote literacy, so I sent a contribution to her foundation. A week or two later, the phone rang, and the voice on the other end said, "Richard, this is Ann Patchett. Are you free for breakfast tomorrow?" Confused about whether I would see her in Nashville or New York, she quickly clarified that she would be in New York for a few hours the next day and wanted to thank me personally for my assistance. She suggested we meet at the St. Regis Hotel at 9 A.M., where we enjoyed a sumptuous breakfast, and she insisted, much like

Jan Morris, that I try the Eggs Benedict. She inquired about my books, asking if I had written anything recently. I explained that I had finished a manuscript for a reader's guide to James Joyce's Ulysses, but I had not been able to find a literary agent to sell it. She replied, "I know just whom to call. Wait until the morning, and I'll have names for you." The next morning, she called with two names.

This meeting took place five years after Edgar died. When I shared what a wonderful person he was and how much I missed him, she asked if I felt lonely. I replied that, yes, I was lonely for good male companionship. She kindly offered to introduce me to her good friend, Jim Fox, who had been a lawyer for a major publishing house and would soon become my close friend. He did admirably as I guided him through a reading of Ulysses, but before he could finish the final chapter, he died in 2024 from cancer at the age of 85.

I encountered nearly all of these remarkable individuals in brief, unexpected meetings, sometimes lasting just a few minutes and other times extending for several hours. Unexpected yet unforgettable, I wouldn't classify them as acquaintances, although a few have become friends. In many instances, it's easy to find the right adjective to capture my impression of each person. Some are remarkable or gracious, while others are generous and kind; at least one is notorious, qualities that are immediately apparent upon meeting them. Some others hide their true selves, for example, by being the person you see on the screen. However, the takeaway for me is that virtually all of them, aside from their talents and accomplishments, are ordinary people.

If you were to ask me if there is someone I would like to meet who is not mentioned here, I would say Orson Welles. I saw him at restaurant tables in both Paris and Beverly Hills, but it was not my style to interrupt a man when he was eating.

Chapter Sixteen:
Moving On

1991-1994

During the early 1980s, I embarked on a new chapter in my career. Although I continued teaching at the College of Staten Island and worked on developing the film studies program, I sensed an uncertain future at the college. I had received tenure and a promotion to Full Professor and was not abandoning the college; however, as an idealist, I grew weary of the turmoil that was undermining our collective dream. Therefore, in addition to teaching, I continued my research and published three more books: Filmguide to "Triumph of the Will" (1975), In the Dark: A Primer for the Movies (1977), and A Peaceable Kingdom: The Shaker Abcedarius, an illustrated children's book (1978), along with a revised and expanded second edition of my first book, Nonfiction Film: A Critical History (1993).

To give myself time to reflect on my future and to create some distance from CSI, I applied for and received a Faculty Fellowship, a position that allowed me to spend a year at the CUNY Central Administrative Office (also referred to as "80th Street"), starting in September 1982. The Central Office was tasked with overseeing and approving various matters, college by college, such as faculty appointments, curriculum development, research grants, and the construction and maintenance of facilities, among other responsibilities, all in accordance with standards set by the Board of Trustees. The Chancellor, Joseph Murphy—previously President of CUNY's Queens College and later the Director of the U. S. Peace Corps operations in Africa—led the Central Office, backed by a team of around eight Vice-Chancellors and ten University Deans. The total staff at 80th Street numbered about 400. The Faculty Fellows observed their work and discussed their plans and projects, thereby giving us a new perspective and understanding of the university, which at the time was the largest public university system in the world. In the 1980s, it comprised 25 colleges, had a budget in the billions, and boasted around 15,000 faculty members alongside hundreds of thousands of students. I was assigned to work with Mary Rothlein, the University Dean for Faculty; however, six months after I began, she resigned to become the Provost of John Jay College of Criminal Justice, CUNY. The Chancellor informed me that, based on Mary's recommendation, he would appoint me as the Acting University Dean for Faculty. Mary and her husband, Leon Goldstein, President of Kingsborough Community College, CUNY, served as my mentors and assisted me in navigating the complexities of the system.

This proved to be a difficult year for me, not only in adjusting to the move from professor to administrator but also in coping with the news that my mother had pancreatic cancer. I took a leave of two weeks to go to Glendale to spend time with her. She could eat only liquids, so I made three different kinds of soup in the hopes that she would enjoy them. At the end of the second week, when I knew she was near death, I asked if she would like any of the soups, and she replied, "Anything but that," perhaps being sarcastic or lightening a moment of great sadness. Whatever, those were her last words as she died minutes later at the age of 68.

Ten years before her death, my father developed an eye disease called macular degeneration, which made it difficult for him to read, write, or drive. He had relied on her to ease his daily life, but my sister Susan, who was very close to him, took her place and was by his side every day. I kept in touch with him through weekly phone calls, which we both looked forward to. Although he remained strong in managing daily life, his near blindness devastated him, and he passed away in 1984.

My father was the most extraordinary man I have ever known: a loving husband, a compassionate father, and a good friend to many admirers. At a memorial gathering in Glendale, friends and family came together to pay their respects. The principal speaker was Paul Hutchinson, his lawyer and neighbor, who spoke about him with great affection. In the past two years, Susan and I experienced the loss of both parents. She had the support of her husband and daughter, while I had the support of my partner Edgar, whose mother had passed away many years earlier and whose father, Walter, would die in 1993. Our fathers, one in California and the other in Pennsylvania had not met yet, but they had regular telephone conversations and arranged to meet in Manhattan to spend a week with their sons. At the last minute, Walter had to cancel the trip due to heart trouble while waiting to board his flight at the Pittsburgh airport. Nevertheless, my father was already on his way to New York. Thus, they never met, and Walter outlived my father by nine years.

I stayed in New York, where, within six months, the Chancellor removed the acting label from my title and appointed me as the University Dean for Faculty and Research. This title came with responsibilities across all CUNY colleges, including the final review and approval of all faculty appointments, promotions, and tenure. Additionally, I served as a liaison with the University Research Foundation, which managed the millions of dollars in research grants earned by the faculty. Throughout this process, I had a keen interest in assisting the colleges in appointing new Distinguished Professors. This promotion could be granted to someone who was already an outstanding faculty member or, preferably, to an impressive scholar or researcher we recruited from another institution. This often meant working closely with potential candidates from outside, encouraging their transition to CUNY, and supporting those who accepted by helping arrange jobs for their spouses, schools for their children, and housing. I enjoyed making these notable individuals feel comfortable and satisfied in their move to CUNY. A Distinguished Professor earned nearly double the salary of a full professor and had a limited teaching schedule. Scientists were provided with all the necessary facilities and staff for their work. Promoting excellence within the extensive faculty was a key goal of the university's mission. We placed special emphasis on publications, exhibitions, research grants, performances, and other accomplishments that brought recognition to the faculty member, their college, and the university.

In 1991, Chancellor Murphy appointed me as his Special Assistant. He expressed a desire to better incorporate the ideas and opinions of the entire university faculty, relying on me, a former faculty member, for assistance. It was remarkable for him to make this effort to engage the faculty more in his work. We met regularly to discuss the issues on which he sought feedback. I visited campuses to speak with people I knew, conferred with the president of the University Senate, which represents the faculty of all colleges, and perhaps most importantly, reassured the faculty union that we were doing this in the best interests of their members.

Although this work was routine, there was also a lighter side to my job. When the Chancellor entertained a notable scholar, politician, or artist, he would invite me to join them for lunch or dinner. This way, I met several distinguished figures, including Harvard economist John Kenneth Galbraith, architecture critic Ada Louise Huxtable, and historian Arthur Schlesinger, Jr. Among the college presidents who visited our offices, my favorite was Vartan Gregorian of Brown University, a fellow Armenian who later became the President of the New York Public Library, where his charm and fundraising skills saved it from financial ruin. Once, Vartan invited me to lunch, and our conversation turned to our favorite writers. He asked if I had read Patrick O'Brian's novels, and I had to admit that I had never heard of them. He shook his head in disbelief and exclaimed, "You call yourself an educated person, and you have never read O'Brian!" After lunch, he asked me to walk him back to his office, but the real reason was to stop at a bookstore, where he bought the first three of the twenty novels in O'Brian's Aubrey/Maturin series. He then handed them to me as a gift and requested a report once I had finished reading. In these novels, the backdrop of the British Royal Navy during the Napoleonic Wars frames the intertwined stories of its two main characters, Commander Jack Aubrey and Dr. Stephen Maturin, his ship's physician. I later took Vartan out to lunch to express how much I enjoyed these books and how grateful I was to him for introducing me to them. As the years have gone by, they have proven to be some of the most significant fiction I have ever read. Indeed, I have read the entire series three times.

University Dean of Executive Search and Evaluation

Chancellor Murphy, who preferred to be called Joe by his colleagues, was pleased with my revitalization of the Distinguished Professor program. The Central Office had neglected these appointments for several years, and Joe admired my success in recruiting outstanding faculty from other institutions. Thus, he asked me to recruit new presidents for the CUNY colleges that needed them, as well as for executive positions at the Central Office. My new title was University Dean for Executive Search and Evaluation, undoubtedly the most challenging assignment I've ever had. My role was twofold: to oversee the searches for new college presidents and Vice Chancellors as well as to evaluate sitting CUNY college presidents who had lost their effectiveness in leading their institutions. When there was a search for a new college president, the final responsibility of the process belonged to the Board of Trustees but was managed by the Chancellor's Office. Both Joe and the Chairperson of the Board wanted a more efficient process than the current one.

Since I had no background in this type of work, I took a crash course to learn the ropes by spending a week in Washington, D.C., at the American Council of Trustees and Alumni, a non-profit organization that specializes in that area. Although the CUNY Board of Trustees already had specific guidelines for its presidential searches, they were outdated and needed revision. Furthermore, there was no sufficient staff in the central office to handle the task. I persuaded Joe that revising the guidelines and establishing a small permanent staff would not only align our system with nationally accepted procedures but also enhance the university's ability to find and hire the best candidates for the positions. I quickly moved into a new office, hired a five-person staff, and got to work.

The search for a new college president is a delicate endeavor in any situation, as it's essential to first earn the trust of the college community involved in the search, including faculty, students, administrative staff, and alumni. I encountered a certain level of wariness, even resentment, when I initiated most of these searches. I was advised to anticipate this. My initial task was to foster their understanding and support by familiarizing them with each step of the process and assuring them that their campus search committee would conduct interviews with potential candidates and provide me with a list of the ten most qualified individuals. I would then visit each candidate's campus to verify their readiness and suitability for the role of college president. This required what lawyers refer to as due diligence. For me, it involved interviews with the college administration as well as a meeting with the editor of the local newspaper to assess any news that could impact the search. I also consulted with the city's Chief of Police. Throughout my tenure in this role, I uncovered information that rendered only three otherwise seemingly suitable candidates unfit for CUNY. One male candidate had been arrested for threatening his wife with a large knife outside their home, an incident witnessed and reported to the police by neighbors. A female candidate, who was already serving as president of her college, was found to be running a student travel program that took most of the students' expenses for her personal gain. The third male candidate, a prominent chemist who won the job, lost it for offering to sell narcotics to faculty members. All of this was confidential, and of course, none of them were aware that I was privy to their secrets.

In 1990, Chancellor Murphy announced his plan to retire. The Board of Trustees asked me to lead the search for candidates eligible to succeed him. This search is more politically driven than that for a college president. Why? CUNY is a public institution where race, gender, and political affiliation, along with academic distinction, achievements, and political skill, play significant roles in selecting a new Chancellor. It is essential for such a candidate to have experience in negotiating with local and state politicians, as CUNY is primarily funded by city and state resources.

After extensive consultations, I compiled a list of six qualified individuals who agreed to be candidates. All our searches were conducted discreetly to protect each candidate's current job and reputation. The Search Committee consisted of representatives from the Trustees, faculty, students, and alumni. While I worked closely with the committee, their efforts were undermined by a former CUNY Chancellor who covertly encouraged them to select his protégé, W. Ann Reynolds, the Chancellor of California State University (CSU), an institution second only to CUNY in size and mission. This was internal interference by someone who, despite having left the Chancellor's office many years ago, continued to attempt to influence university affairs. It called into question the legitimacy of the search. Nevertheless, we proceeded with the review process, including a personal, on-site visit to evaluate the candidate's current situation. Two members of our Board of Trustees accompanied me on a three-day trip to Los Angeles. We spoke with Reynolds, her key staff members, and three sitting presidents of Cal State colleges. We discovered that she had a hard-driving, often autocratic administrative style that led to significant conflict within the academic community and raised concerns among politicians across the State of California. As we prepared to leave for home, we were shocked to learn that the CSU Board of Trustees had just fired her. She should have informed me immediately so that we could assess whether she was still a viable candidate, but this was never mentioned during our final one-on-one interview that day. Her honesty was questionable. On the return flight, the two CUNY trustees and I concurred that Reynolds was not the right fit for the position.

The Search Committee had not yet had the opportunity to interview Reynolds because she said she claimed that she was too busy to make the trip. Apparently, she felt certain to get the job with her mentor's backing. However, she flew into New York for a one-night stay, giving the search committee only a few hours to interview. I was at that meeting, of course, and astonished at how weakly she made a case for her selection. Afterward, the committee asked me to review her record but not to express an opinion. Several Trustees complained that they did not have sufficient time to talk with her, but the meeting proceeded, and with a very close vote, they voted to hire her. This was 1990. From the moment she settled into her office, she caused problems rather than made progress. Early on, it was noted by those of us with whom she worked closely that she signed her memos with her WAR (her initials), which was a cautionary sign to us all. Seven turbulent years later, the CUNY Board fired her for the same reasons as did Cal State.

Provost at Pratt Institute

I remained in my position, working amicably with Chancellor Reynolds. She seemed to like me, and I liked her as well. However, I had grown weary of managing searches and wished to return to the academic life of a Provost at a college in the New York area. I discussed this with her, and she graciously supported me with a kind letter of recommendation. At that time, the only such job available was at Pratt Institute in Brooklyn. Founded in 1887, Pratt is a respected private college specializing in art, engineering, architecture, and library science. The mission of the founder, Charles Pratt, an oil tycoon who did not attend college, was to provide men and women, especially women, with the opportunity to learn an art or skill that would enable them to improve their lives. Indeed, it was one of the first institutions of higher education in the U.S. that welcomed all people, regardless of gender, age, class, or color. Pratt offered four-year baccalaureate programs not only in fine arts, architecture, engineering, and library science and technology but also graduate programs in the arts. It sounds promising on paper, but Pratt appeared to the larger academic community to be in serious trouble.

Traditionally, a college provost is the chief academic administrator and often serves as the deputy to the president. After applying for the Pratt position, I prepared for a possible interview by first visiting Pratt's park-like campus. The grounds were well maintained, but the college buildings, dating back to the 19th century, required modernization. The students on campus seemed content, but I left my visit feeling that something was amiss. After speaking with various colleagues at CUNY, I learned that the college was struggling to attract new students and, consequently, faced serious financial difficulties. Despite high tuition, the funds were not allocated to maintaining and upgrading the college's facilities. For instance, the administrative computer system, essential for modern management, was completely outdated. We joked that it was the only steam-powered computer still in use. During interviews, I talked with staff, faculty, and students, but they seemed unable to provide any useful information. I already knew that Pratt had historically been run at the top level more as a family philanthropy than as an academic institution. In fact, nearly all its former presidents had been Pratt males, and most Board of Trustees members were either Pratts or married to them. The most recent president, Richardson Pratt, Jr., held the position for 18 years. Charles Pratt, the founder, established the management style that followed. Subsequent presidents ran the college with a firm but generous hand, using their personal finances to erase budget deficits. However, the institution needed more than financial generosity and its stellar reputation to attract prospective students; it required sound academic and financial leadership. Richardson Pratt retired in 1990 and was succeeded by Warren F. Ilchman, a political economist who had previously served as the Provost of the Rockefeller College of Public Affairs and Policy at SUNY Albany and thus lacked experience in leading any college, especially one focused on the arts.

My friends and colleagues tried to dissuade me from applying for the job, but I went ahead and applied anyway. I needed to start my new career somewhere, and I was intrigued by the idea of working at a college of the arts. For one thing, I saw an enormous opportunity for a new filmmaking program. Since my personal life was in Manhattan, I had to look for jobs in the nearby area. Consequently, I was interviewed by the Pratt search committee. Although they skillfully avoided my questions about the new president, I sensed their disapproval of him, which made them cautious in selecting a provost.

I wanted to discuss the situation with the administrative staff. I had a polite conversation with the current acting provost, who had no academic background and was merely filling in until someone was hired. I was informed that the chief financial officer was not available for a meeting with me, and I received the same response when I tried to meet with the Dean of Student Recruitment and Enrollment. Someone, likely Ilchman, was blocking my effort to gather the information I needed to keep my interest in the position. Given my experience with executive searches, I considered this operation to be poorly managed at best. Still, with little knowledge about the institution, I was then interviewed by President Ilchman.

Apparently, he was chosen to be Pratt's president because of his social credentials and connections rather than his talents or achievements. He graduated from Brown University and earned his Ph.D. from Cambridge University. His wife, who was then president of Sarah Lawrence College, appeared to be his only advisor. In fact, he relied heavily on her experience, often incorrectly comparing the two institutions. My first meeting with him was not a success; he was focused on my personal life—he seemed more impressed with Edgar's position at the Frick than my qualifications for the position. Although the search committee had already recommended to the Board of Trustees that I be hired, I was astonished that none of the Board's members interviewed me.

A week later, Ilchman and I had dinner at the University Club, where after he had three martinis, he got to the point and offered me the job. The salary and other benefits were lower than what I was paid at CUNY, but I managed to persuade him to make them at least equal. I requested a college car for my daily commute from Manhattan to Brooklyn, but he declined to let me use one of the available ones. By then, I was understandably discouraged and said I needed time to consider his offer. He drove me home and, as I got out of the car, said, "We'll make a wonderful team."

Once again, my friends urged me not to take the job due to Pratt's financial issues. Bernard Harleston, a former president of CCNY who knew Ilchman during their time at SUNY Albany, advised against accepting the position, suggesting it might harm my reputation when I sought a better job later on. However, I viewed it as a challenge to address the issues all college provosts are hired to face. After a week or so, and stubborn as I was, I accepted the job. In hindsight, I can honestly say that working alongside Warren Ilchman taught me valuable lessons about what not to do as a college president.

Before starting at Pratt, I needed a break, so Edgar and I took a delightful two-week trip to the Dominican Republic. On August 1, 1991, I began my role as Provost of Pratt Institute. During my two years there, I implemented many essential changes and improvements, as well as made some mistakes. One of the most challenging tasks was developing the plan to close the School of Engineering, as sanctioned by the President and Trustees. I believed I had created a thorough plan, but Warren never asked to discuss it because I think he knew it would be difficult for everyone involved and didn't want to face blame. I had to act quickly because we were informed that the program was set to lose its professional accreditation at the end of the academic year. Warren was astonished when I negotiated the transfer of four hundred Pratt engineering students to two local institutions, with a commitment that Pratt would cover their first year's tuition. The twelve remaining Engineering faculty members presented the biggest challenge since the school's failure was largely their responsibility, which they refused to admit. We retired several of them with a payout equivalent to two years of salary, transferred one to the Pratt School of Architecture, and helped the others find jobs elsewhere—a difficult undertaking.

I faced other significant problems, particularly regarding computer use by faculty, staff, and students. In several academic departments, faculty members were hesitant to learn how to utilize computers in their teaching and for their students. If they had been interested, they would have recognized that proficiency in computers was crucial for positions in the arts and design fields. A few phone calls confirmed that our main competitors—the Rhode Island School of Design and the California Institute of the Arts—had integrated student computer use years earlier. I spoke with executives at Apple, who generously offered free computers for our students and faculty, along with training from their staff. However, most faculty members rejected my proposal and this offer. Some were skeptical about computers, some were too hesitant to learn a completely new technology, some resisted acquiring the knowledge necessary to equip their students with the skills they needed in the "real" world, and a few were nearing retirement and indifferent to the situation.

I initiated discussions with the Chancellor's Office about a plan to acquire Pratt Institute as a CUNY institution. The main reason for this was that while there were art programs in all the colleges, there was no specific college of art. It would be fitting to have a public arts college with tuition 80% lower than Pratt's. Such a vibrant college—named Pratt/CUNY College of the Arts—would attract students from various NYC high schools focused on art education. CUNY could purchase the Brooklyn property, construct new buildings, and renovate old ones because it had access to the funds necessary to restore Pratt to its former status and reputation. CUNY officials supported the idea, but Ilchman did not and discouraged the Pratt Board of Trustees from examining the proposal and engaging in discussions about it. As for creative thinking, I remember that Ilchman was exploring fundraising by renting the soon empty Engineering building to the New York College of Podiatric Medicine. Their sign on one of the buildings of an arts college sent entirely the wrong signals. He ultimately abandoned the idea.

Despite all this, a silver lining emerged from my work at Pratt. In collaboration with the Vice President for Finance, we implemented various policies that helped cut spending and reduce the budget deficit. Financial records had not been systematically maintained, so we introduced a computer program to rectify that. Many faculty salaries were inconsistent with the union contract, indicating that the Deans were making decisions without adhering to the rules. With the cooperation of the union representative, we addressed this issue and eliminated several overpaid salaries. However, unprofessional and occasionally illegal activities were taking place on campus. To further investigate Pratt's financial situation, I requested an independent CPA to review the books from the past ten years. He uncovered questionable activities. For instance, every one of those years, and likely even before, there was an annual charge of $60,000 for floor wax. Since the Pratt buildings did not have wooden floors, what was all this wax being used for? Who was behind this scheme? Through hidden video cameras, we discovered that a monthly shipment of wax was delivered to the loading dock, after which the perpetrator, the head of the school security office, had each shipment immediately loaded into his trucks and driven away. He sold the wax and pocketed the profits. We agreed not to press charges if he resigned immediately.

Working at Pratt was the challenge I desired, but I could no longer tolerate the faculty's stubborn resistance to change, the Board of Trustees' reluctance to secure the necessary funding for such changes, or the alumni organization's lack of interest in protecting their college. It felt almost as if they wanted the college to close. Therefore, at the end of my academic year, I submitted my resignation to the president, who accepted it. At the conclusion of my final week, I received a shocking surprise when I went to retrieve my car and drive home. It was then dark when I was attacked by an unidentified person. Whether this individual intended to kill me or not, I was not injured. The Pratt neighborhood was dangerous, yet no one there had anything against me. Who fired that gun? It could have come from some disturbed individual within the college gates. Regardless, the police could not identify any suspects. By the end of the following year, I learned that the Pratt Board of Trustees had requested Ilchman's resignation.

Returning to the Central Office

Since I needed to find a new job immediately, I called Chancellor Reynolds to see if she might take me back on her staff, and she promptly offered me a position as her "special assistant." I enjoyed being back at CUNY because it gave me time to consider my next move. By mid-year, I decided to return to teaching. I remained aware that the Chancellor was having a tough time, to the extent that The New York Times described her as a "hard-charging, sometimes tyrannical administrator who can be utterly charming but also short-tempered and brusque." After leading CUNY for seven turbulent years, the feisty Chancellor was eventually fired by The Board of Trustees.

Professor of Film Studies at Hunter College/CUNY

In 1994, I realized how much I had missed teaching, even though I enjoyed my years in administration. I knew some of the film studies faculty at Hunter College, and after inquiring about available positions, they hired me as a tenured full professor. I recognized that the film program and its faculty needed motivation, but my focus was solely on teaching, and I was happy with my students. I taught Introduction to Film, which led to the writing and publication of my textbook, Looking at Movies, now in its 8th edition and widely used in hundreds of colleges. I also created and taught a course on Cinematic Space and another on John Ford's films and was asked to revive the required course, Close Film Analysis, dedicating it to Orson Welles's Citizen Kane.

After seven years, I retired at 63. The students in my Citizen Kane class threw me a party where they screened their short spoof of Welles's movie with me as the subject. I was touched by their talent, friendship, and genuine love for film. I retired not because I was tired of teaching but because I could focus on planning and writing the textbook mentioned above. My contract with W. W. Norton allowed me a year to submit the finished manuscript. I had already moved into an apartment at the Barclay, where I converted the second bedroom into an office that could hold my thousands of books and other office essentials.

Edgar, who had retired from the Frick two years earlier, supported me throughout the activities of the past nine years, including my transitions from CUNY to Pratt, then back to CUNY, and finally to Hunter. He was enjoying his retirement but kept a small office at the Frick, where he worked as an art consultant for collectors and museums in the U.S. and abroad. Happiness and kindness continued to thrive in our relationship.

Chapter Seventeen:
Life With Edgar

Who's Edgar When He's at Home?

You already know that Edgar was an art historian and museum curator, but you might ask, as the Irish do, "Who's he when he's at home?" As someone who knew him well, I can say he was consistently gentle, kind, thoughtful, and charming, whether at work, at home, or with friends. He chose his friends carefully, aiming for long-lasting relationships, and generally remained loyal to them. While he may have preferred male friends, we often spent time with women. Of course, he had his faults, but they rarely bothered me, as we usually resolved them before they escalated into problems. At work, as in life, he was a perfectionist who set high standards for everything he did and for everyone who entered his life.

At home—which broadly means our two apartments—he was a gracious host and a master of French cooking. For our dinners with guests, we enjoyed creating menu cards to announce the meal. I printed them on the computer, and he contributed one of his drawings. He truly loved greeting and entertaining guests, who were always happy to receive an invitation. In the early 1990s, he redesigned his dining room to resemble a French bistro, with mirrors on all the walls, a comfortable banquette, a new dining table, and swinging doors leading to the kitchen. This way, he was never far from his guests while cooking. It was unusual for an ordinary Manhattan apartment to have such a welcoming and splendid space for enjoying food, drink, and conversation. After his death, when the apartment was emptied, a crew came in and demolished the room.

When we visited friends, he often became the center of attention since those in the art world were always interested in general gossip and what was happening at the Frick. He shared delightful stories about the people we met on our trips, often bringing them to life with his talent for mimicking how some individuals spoke. His mimicry could be kind and gentle or sharp and cynical, much like the various drawings he created for his journals. There are thirty-three of these books—drawings by him and text by me—carefully preserved and accessible at the Frick Art Reference Library.

I wouldn't be honest in this brief description of his character if I didn't mention that he also removed people from his life by sentencing them to Thorn Ridge, located on Rattlesnake Road in the Connecticut hills. It is entirely an imaginary place that we created for people who annoyed us with their bad behavior. One might assume that Thorn Ridge is a large institution; in reality, it is quite small, indeed invisible. There were two forms of punishment at Thorn Ridge: a short-term sentence or, worst of all, solitary confinement, which, like a prison term, is reserved for those who will never return to civilized life. In truth, all of this existed in our minds, and there was only one person we sentenced to solitary confinement.

You might ask me, "What was your relationship with Edgar?" Without pause, I would answer that, in our troubled world, it was almost unbelievably amiable. In forty years, we never had any kind of argument or fight. Hard to believe, but true. Disagreement, surely, but even Though we saw things differently on some issues, we respected one another and found ways to get along since the day we met. However, there was one issue on which we disagreed. I wanted to have a country house where we could spend weekends, but Edgar's only response was, "Remember Clockwork Orange." Those who remember Stanley Kubrick's film will recall that a key scene involved hoodlums went broke into a famous writer's country house, beating him and raping his wife. I never got my country house.

Edgar was at his best when we traveled, which was a significant part of our life together. It's often said that travel can bring out the best and worst in people, and it certainly brought out the best in both of us. I planned the itineraries for our trips while a travel agent handled the reservations. Edgar trusted my judgment in selecting all the necessary details involving the many museums, restaurants, and hotels where we stayed. Wherever we went, Edgar and I were the perfect travel companions and life partners.

Dogs

Writing about my life with Edgar wouldn't feel complete without mentioning our dogs. While Edgar never had a dog before he met me, I couldn't imagine living in a world without dogs. However, as a child, my parents saw dogs as a nuisance, while I viewed them as family members. Neither my father nor my mother had ever owned a pet dog prior to my request for one. Nevertheless, they kindly gave me my first dog when I was about 10, a rescue fox terrier we named Bumpy. The name fits well because he had vision problems and would bump into doors, walls, and people as if he couldn't see them. That didn't bother me; he was a lovable little guy who followed me everywhere. However, my mother was frustrated because he dug holes in her garden, destroyed plants, and pooped on the lawn, making clean-up necessary. Like most terriers, he didn't like being restrained and tragically broke loose, running into the street where he was hit by a car. I didn't find out about it for several hours, during which my mother, trying to shield me from the news, suggested I walk around the neighborhood to see if I could find him. So, I wandered around, calling his name and asking neighbors if they had seen him. It was a fruitless search, and only after my father came home did she admit that the dog had been killed by a car and that I would find him in a box in the garage. I wanted to bury him in the backyard, but instead, my parents took him to the city dog pound for cremation.

After we moved to the new house, I got my second rescue dog, a fully-grown collie we named Lucky. He was surprisingly gentle for his size and a great friend to children. At a neighborhood party for people and their dogs, he won six cans of dog food for having the longest tail among the canine contestants. Lucky, like Bumpy, caused damage to the garden, yet my mother tried to get along with him. As I recall, he made unwanted visits to my school. I worked hard to train him to be a better dog, but he met his fate after digging up some of my mother's prized roses. She took him to the dog pound and asked to have him "put to sleep," the sickening phrase used at that time. I learned this when I came home from school that day. I cried for hours and refused to eat dinner with the family. Later, my father brought a tray of food to my room and tried to calm me. I was furious that my mother made such a decision without consulting me, which created another rift between us. After that, we had cats as pets, but unfortunately, for all their charms, cats are not dogs.

Fortunately, after moving to New York, I was free to do as I pleased regarding dogs. Edgar and I decided to get a Jack Russell Terrier and visited a New Jersey family that had puppies for sale. From just a few weeks old, Edgar took a liking to one of them, so we brought him home and named him Spot due to the large black spot on his otherwise all-white coat. Spot was truly mine because I raised him in my apartment, fed him, cleaned up after him, taught him how to walk on city streets, and took him to Central Park nearly every day. He lived with me. Edgar claimed co-ownership because he loved the dog, but he really wasn't capable of all the duties involved. Anyone who has known a Jack Russell Terrier knows they possess an inexhaustible supply of energy. Spot fit that description perfectly, but he was also an unusually sensitive, gentle dog who showed emotion when upset. He didn't like being left alone, which I, of course, had to do when I went to work. To make it up to him, I tried to take him to the park whenever I could.

As for Central Park, that's where I met Luiz Bocchi walking his miniature brown poodle, Patrick. Spot immediately adopted Patrick as his best friend, so Luiz and I made it a point to meet at the same time every afternoon to keep the dogs happy. But this is about Spot. Jack Russell terriers prefer sleeping with their owner; in my case, he sleeps on top of my head. Spot would wait for me to get into bed, then jump up to join me, maneuvering into position on the pillow. He then curled around the contour of my head and promptly went to sleep. He did this every night, even when we traveled. If I got up at night to use the bathroom, he followed me there, waiting patiently, and then resumed his position, keeping my bald head warm. We took him to Fire Island one weekend, and he got his first look at and taste of the ocean. I took him out into the water to see if he would swim, but an unexpected wave tossed him back onto the shore, where he landed with a thud. Spot didn't like that; he was unusually sensitive and ignored me for a few days. After that experience, he never liked being near water.

When I left Spot alone in the apartment, I assumed he would spend most of his time sleeping. However, one day I was confronted by the woman who lived above me, a particularly nasty person who claimed that the dog cried all day, which annoyed her. I asked my next-door neighbor if she had heard the dog crying, and she replied that she had never heard a peep out of him. So, I hired a dog walker to take him out daily for an hour, knowing this would please him. One afternoon, while walking him myself, I noticed he was trying to cough up something he might have swallowed. I knew dogs could clear their digestive systems by eating grass, so I took him to the park, where there was plenty of grass. After he ate enough grass to make him vomit, we walked back to the apartment. He didn't eat his dinner and was obviously in pain again, so I took him to the emergency room at the Animal Medical Center. After an examination, a doctor came out to say they had found in his system "enough rat poison to kill a horse." He explained that a dog would typically avoid poison, suggesting that someone must have forced the food on him. I suspected the woman upstairs, but without evidence, I couldn't do anything about the situation, so Spot was cremated, and his ashes were buried in a friend's garden.

Soon, I was ready to have another dog—a Jack Russell, of course—and checked out the kennels that specialized in that breed. We visited a kennel in Greenwich, Connecticut, owned by the president of the Jack Russell Terrier Club of America. Beforehand, I called him and explained that I wanted a pet that wouldn't be afraid of the city. He said he had just the right dog. When we got out of the car, we saw the kennels about 200 feet away. The owner waved us over, and no sooner had we started than a young terrier named Dylan bolted across the grass and leaped right into Edgar's arms. Just as Spot had chosen Edgar, Dylan did the same. The owner told us that Dylan was the only male in a litter of female puppies who tormented him and made his life miserable. He had tried to escape. Dylan was a fully pedigreed dog, clearly raised in the best conditions but in need of a new home. The three of us happily drove back into town. Although he was possessive of us both, he lived with me. I never thought for a moment to change his name.

Dylan had no trouble acclimating to the city and especially loved our daily walks in Central Park, where we played one-on-one dog soccer, which was essentially me throwing a tennis ball as far as I could and him eagerly fetching it back for another round. In Spot's tradition, he quickly made friends with Patrick, my friend Luiz's poodle. I was working at Pratt Institute in Brooklyn and didn't get home until around 6, so I hired a dog walker to give Dylan a long walk each day. When I arrived home, he was the happiest little terrier in New York, following me from room to room, getting underfoot in the kitchen when I was trying to prepare dinner, and generally begging for my full attention. On the nights we had dinner at Edgar's, Dylan, of course, came along. He loved Edgar almost as much as he loved me.

Dylan traveled with us to Europe three times and was mostly a good boy, adjusting easily to the long ride in a dog crate in the airplane's baggage hold. On land, he followed us everywhere, and in France, he joined us in restaurants that allowed dogs. In June 1996, we returned to France and rented a house in Versailles as our base for exploring the South of France. The property featured a fenced-in garden that was perfect for Dylan. However, a very disagreeable neighbor didn't like the dog and called the owner of the house, threatening to kill the dog if we didn't leave. He may have been bluffing, but his presence posed a threat to Dylan's life. So, we left, but before that, I booked hotels for the remaining time on our itinerary, selecting only those that allowed dogs. While in a restaurant, Dylan politely sat under the table and enjoyed the food we selected for him from the doggie menu. A waiter once asked him if he preferred green beans or carrots with his veal patty.

Back in Manhattan, Edgar occasionally took Dylan to work with him on Mondays when the museum was closed. On his first visit, the dog escaped from Edgar's office, ran down the stairs to the garden court, and jumped into the fountain pool, swimming back and forth until someone retrieved him. He loved swimming and, unlike Spot, never passed a body of water he didn't want to jump into, including the fountains in front of the Metropolitan Museum. We spent many weekends at Channing Blake's country house in Pawling, upstate New York. Channing was a landscape architect, and as a hobby, he bred miniature, short-haired Dachshunds that got along beautifully with Dylan. The large property featured three ponds, each approximately 40 ft. x 60 ft. and about 4 feet deep. Wild geese came and went from the pond closest to the house, which was Dylan's favorite. When he grew exhausted from chasing those birds, who simply flew away when he got too close, I waded into the water to bring the tired dog out, toweled him dry, and left him to sleep in front of the living room fireplace.

When he was twelve, Dylan developed a condition that made it impossible for him to control his bladder. His veterinarian said there was no cure for it and that it would likely worsen, so in 2001, we decided to have him euthanized. Our friend Henrietta Suhr, another landscape specialist with a large estate in Mt. Kisco, offered to bury Dylan's ashes in his favorite spot in her garden. Dylan was the perfect example of a Jack Russell Terrier: energetic, loyal, and loving.

Traveling Together

One could say that travel defined Edgar and me, both as individuals and as a couple, but, anyway, as I said previously, it brought out the best in us both. We traveled frequently, both to foreign countries and in the USA, together or solo. The solo trips were related to our jobs. We visited France more than any other place, simply because Edgar knew the country so well, including the best hotels and restaurants or that small French city where he knew a museum that he knew I would like. Over the years, he had made many lasting friends who welcomed us into their homes on each trip. My diaries and his drawing books show that we traveled together to France more than twenty times in forty years; during the same time, he traveled there alone on business fifteen more times and once to Russia, where he negotiated a rare loan of drawings from the State Hermitage Museum in Saint Petersburg for an exhibition at the Frick.

While we ordinarily stayed in hotels, in 1990, we rented a house located in Aix-en-Provence at the base of the Montagne St.-Victoire, known as Cezanne's Mountain, because it appears in so many of his landscape paintings. The town of Aix was a thirty-minute drive away. Soon after arriving with Spot, we drove into town to shop at the outdoor market. Soon, we saw people pointing at the mountain, where a forest fire had ignited very close to our house. As it raged on, firefighters closed the road, forcing us to find a room in a local hotel for the night. The next day, we returned to find that this devastating fire had destroyed many houses, but fortunately, ours was spared; however, it did ruin the poolside furniture and all the vegetation in the large garden. The neighbors were not so lucky; the closest one lost ten horses in the flames. I regretted leaving Aix, a charming town with a fantastic public market where we shopped several times a week. Dylan became somewhat of a star, charming the farmers who brought their produce and other food for sale. In fact, he was so popular that several of them always had a special food gift for him.

Before leaving Aix, we had lunch with friends Edgar had met through the Rothschilds. They were returning to Paris and offered to lend us their house as guests for the rest of our trip. We couldn't arrange that, so they accepted my suggestion to return the following summer for two weeks. The property, a working vineyard named Le Domaine Saint-Joseph, sat on an 800-acre estate surrounded by vines and was accessed through an arched gateway. The house itself, perched atop a hill, was a ten-bedroom mansion that also faced the Montagne St.-Victoire. The grounds featured a swimming pool, a large chapel now used by the owner as his painting studio, and serene areas that offered perfect silence for meditative walks. The buildings were originally part of a monastery, and the grounds included a small graveyard for priests. It was all ours, except for a few days when Andrew and Gaby Bordwin, friends from New York, came to stay. Andrew, a well-known professional photographer, took pictures of the place and, when we returned, presented us with a leather-bound volume of them. The only other people around the estate were a weekly housekeeper, a gardener, and a 24-hour watchman whose companion was a friendly German Shepherd named Aquilla, who took a special liking to Spot and followed him everywhere he went.

Our visits to grand vacation homes were not just confined to France. Berthe David-Weill invited us to stay at La Caracola in a village perched high on a bluff along the Costa Brava, just a few miles south of the border between Spain and France. Besides her main residences in Paris and New York, Berthe owned vacation homes in Spain, Venice, and Greenwich, Connecticut. The name La Caracola translates to snail shell in English. Berthe remodeled an older house to incorporate the sea-shell motif to create a retreat for herself and her lover. The walled estate features a vast lawn dotted with towering cedar trees. In contrast, the house itself is small and intimate, with one bedroom and one guest room.

One of the delights on the grounds was a glass pavilion resembling a seashell, where rare shells were displayed in glass cabinets. The furniture, also shaped like seashells, echoed this motif, A large swimming pool, hidden away in a grove of cypress trees, provided the ideal setting for nude swimming. There was little need to leave the estate, except for a short trip to the nearby Salvador Dali Theater and Museum or for shopping in the village. We stayed for four nights, but since there was only one guest room, already occupied by one of Berthe's friends, we were accommodated in a hotel near the house. Berthe brought her French chef along for her travels to her residences, ensuring the meals were superb. Her personal chauffeur, who had driven her from Paris, was gladly at our service for the little sightseeing we did. One night, we had to decline his persistent offer to take us to a local bar that was frequented by gays and drag queens.

In 1983, which Edgar called Annus Mirabilis (Wonderful Year), we enjoyed memorable experiences on a trip between Paris and the Perigord and Quercy regions of Southwest France. In Paris, Berthe entertained us and one day sent us off in her chauffeured Mercedes to visit Giverny, Claude Monet's house and garden in Normandy. Her Italian driver was a true romantic who played tapes of Puccini's opera at full volume in the car. On another afternoon, he drove us to meet one of Berthe's remarkable friends, the Comtesse de Billy-Fenaille. She welcomed us at the Chateau de Billy, which she had shared with the Comte de Billy until his death; he was a friend of Marcel Proust and the French ambassador to both Japan and Greece. We were not only sent to meet her but also to learn about an amazing secret. During World War II, the treasures of the Louvre were removed and stored for safekeeping among various grand houses, including hers. The proud Madame la Comtesse took us to the cellar to show us where, during World War II, the Louvre had hidden Leonardo da Vinci's "Mona Lisa" behind a false wall. The Louvre systematically moved treasures like these from one safe house to another to avoid discovery by the Nazis.

Baron Elie and Baroness Liliane de Rothschild became good friends, and we enjoyed their warm hospitality, impressive art collection, and exceptional meals. Baron Elie, who had been imprisoned by the Nazis, was a sportsman known for telling the funniest, dirtiest jokes, while Liliane was a patron of French art and fashion. Karl Lagerfeld was one of her closest friends; not only did he design her clothes, but he also sent her a dozen roses every day—yes, every day she was in Paris. To celebrate her birthday, Elie organized a party to be held not at their Paris house but at their country residence, Royaumont, a former abbey near Chantilly. We planned to drive there, but I decided against it, so Liliane simply called her good friend Hubert de Givenchy, another guest, and asked him to take us in his car. Edgar sat up front with the designer, a shy man of few words, but they found common ground discussing French paintings. The party itself was a gala sit-down dinner for the crème de la crème of Paris society, preceded by cocktails on the terrace and concluding with a fireworks display. Everything about the evening reflected the Rothschild style of elegance, beauty, and pleasure.

During our 2005 trip to Germany, we sought out places we hadn't visited before, such as Berlin's Holocaust Memorial, the Jewish Museum, and the restored dome of the Reichstag. We attended a performance by the Berlin Philharmonic in its impressive Concert Hall, accompanied by Buddy Giovinazzi and his wife, Gesine. Buddy, my former student, now living in Berlin, had become a well-regarded movie director. In Dresden, we enjoyed a private tour with the curator of the old masters' gallery at the Zwinger Museum and afterward took an elevator inside the completely reconstructed Frauenkirche for a bird's eye view of the restored church. In Nürnberg, I saw the ruins of the former Reichspartag Stadium, where Leni Riefenstahl made the propaganda film Triumph of the Will, which I had written a book about. The site had suffered significant demolition, but enough remained to make it worth the visit. On another day, we relished the chance to see the interior of the Wies Kirche, a rococo church near

Neuschwanstein, Ludwig II's storybook castle, which we also visited. Back in Munich, we reunited with our friend Manu von Miller, Edgar's protégée, with whom we explored another Baroque masterpiece, the Asamkirche. Whenever we're in Munich, we always visit the Glyptothek (sculpture gallery), renowned for its remarkable collection of Greek and Roman antiquities, including the breathtaking sculpture known as the Barberini Faun. In 2007, we embarked on a two-week driving trip through Spain, awestruck by the Alhambra, captivated by the Museo Prado, which we visited for the second time together, and ultimately were thrilled in Córdoba, where Edgar witnessed and loved his first bullfight.

While we had several pleasant trips to Switzerland, the next one wasn't enjoyable, but it certainly was memorable. In 1981, we began in Zurich and then moved on to Bürgenstock, known primarily for its famous hotel, the Bürgenstock Resort. It is perched on top of a high ridge, offering impressive views of Lake Lucerne and the surrounding mountains. Driving up to the hotel can be tricky, so the hotel recommends parking in the lot at the base of the hill and utilizing the hotel's car service and driver to navigate the winding road. What we found, as we were soon to discover, was that despite its magnificent location, this was, as they say, the hotel from hell. Upon arriving at the front desk, we were informed that they had not received our reservation, which I clarified by presenting the acknowledgment I had received weeks before. Next, we were told there was no available accommodation unless we were willing to share a cramped room with two beds, clearly intended for staff. They made it abundantly clear that we were not welcome when Edgar overheard a clerk refer to us as the German equivalent of "dirty men." All this was difficult to comprehend, for we were two well-dressed men who had arrived in a rented Mercedes sedan. Moreover, I mentioned that my parents had vacationed there and recommended it. But we both suspected that we were the victims of homophobia, which is nearly unheard of in Switzerland, a country where gay culture and gay individuals have been accepted virtually everywhere, including Lucerne, since the 1940s. What else could explain the rude and undoubtedly illegal treatment we endured?

It was late in the afternoon, and since it might have been difficult to find a comparable hotel, we decided to spend the night. They made a similar fuss over our request for a table in the then-famous restaurant but ultimately agreed to give us a nice table in the middle of the room. After a glass of champagne and much discussion about the superb menu, I chose a veal chop with a sauce of wild mushrooms, cream, and Madeira wine for my main course—a classic Swiss dish—accompanied by Rösti, the nation's favorite potato dish. After the first course was taken away and the main course placed before me, I cut off a piece of veal, covered it with the thick sauce, and began to eat. Suddenly, I spit out shards of red glass into a napkin, probably from a broken wine bottle. My mouth wasn't cut, but I could have been seriously injured. After examining the rest of the dish and gathering a pile of sharp glass pieces, we signaled the Maître d'hôtel, who offered no explanation or apology and asked what I would like as a replacement. The glass didn't seem to bother him at all. I chose a grilled steak and a potato dish, neither of which contained glass. The waiters acted as if nothing out of the ordinary had happened. This restaurant was a disaster, as was the entire hotel.

The next morning, we woke up early, skipped breakfast, and were driven back down the mountain to our car by a sullen driver who didn't utter a word. Before arriving here, we had visited the Berghof in Austria, Adolf Hitler's vacation home in the Bavarian Alps near Berchtesgaden. As we stepped out of the car, the driver remained silent, but when I said, "Goodbye, Berchtesgaden," which was the name of Hitler's mountain retreat, he shot me a hateful look that I still remember. Suggesting that the hotel had Nazi ties gave me a strong, albeit childish feeling that I had reciprocated the hotel's rude treatment of us.

Over the years, we took trips to Turkey, Greece, Poland, Hungary, and the Czech Republic, as well as Ireland, Norway, Denmark, and Sweden. On this side of the Atlantic, we visited Mexico, the Dominican Republic, Puerto Rico, Martinique, St. Bart's, and Canada. In the USA, we traveled, either solo or together, to forty-seven of the fifty states. And of the great national parks in this country, we visited Yosemite, Yellowstone, and the Grand Tetons; Bryce, Zion, Monument Valley, and Grand Canyon; as well as Niagara Falls. Edgar enjoyed the monochrome desert parks more than the greenery of Yosemite or Yellowstone. I will long remember the Rothko Chapel in Houston, an architectural and spiritual experience, as well as our tour of Frank Lloyd Wright's houses in Chicago and Louis Kahn's library at the Exeter Academy in New Hampshire. In

1994, we sailed to England in first class on the QE2 and flew home on the supersonic aircraft Concorde.

Of all these travels, our second favorite destination, after France, was India, a country we visited five times, with each trip lasting about five weeks. I had loved the country since childhood. My mother read me children's books about India, and much later, I read both fiction and nonfiction set in the country, expanded my familiarity with Indian movies, and tried to learn as much as I could about Indian literature, art, and music. Initially, Edgar wasn't keen on going to India. He had the ridiculous excuse that since there were no 18th-century French paintings to see there, he didn't understand why he should go. Knowing that he was joking and would eventually give in, I made him an offer he couldn't refuse: if he didn't like it after the first week, I would pay for his return travel and continue the trip by myself. He agreed.

On the first morning, we arrived in Bombay (now Mumbai) via London. After checking into the grand Taj Mahal Palace Hotel, I took a short nap. Edgar decided to go for a walk and experience his first glimpse of India. So far, so good. I slept for about two hours, and when he returned, he shook me awake and said, "You won't believe your eyes. I love it!" The rest of the trip had its usual snags and disappointments, mostly late or canceled flights, but overall, it proved to be nearly perfect. In fact, after we returned to New York, I started planning our second trip, which we took two years later.

And then the third, fourth, and fifth to different regions, all by private car and driver since foreigners are not allowed to drive there. Varanasi (formerly Benares) is a truly special place in a country full of countless wonders. We visited it on each trip; it's a location one never forgets. It is one of the most sacred cities in Hinduism, where devout pilgrims come to purify themselves by bathing in the Ganges. After death, bodies are cremated on large outdoor pyres, and the ashes are scattered into the great river. Edgar was so touched by the funeral rites that he said if he died first, I should return with his ashes and scatter them in the Ganges. As you will read in the next chapter, that's exactly what I did.

Our first trip to India included a week in Nepal, highlighted by a plane trip that circled the top of Mount Everest, and on our fourth trip, we went to Sri Lanka, with its impressive tea plantations and outstanding Elephant Sanctuary, where we watched a mother and father elephant teach their infants how to swim in the river. Imagine teaching a 450-pound animal to swim. Both states are now countries independent from India, one at the top of the map of India, the other an island at the bottom. For the last trip together, we spent our fifth trip at Wildflower Hall, a hotel with a magnificent view of the Himalayas, where we enjoyed the Christmas and New Year's holidays. I fell in love with the place when I found a notice in our room that said: "Please keep the window closed during the day to safeguard your belongings from monkeys." While it's a legitimate warning—monkeys are ravenous thieves—it is also an example of Indian humor.

In 2015, I made a month-long solo trip to Japan. Edgar decided to stay at home. Having a whole month and taking advantage of the amazing Japanese train system, I visited all the major cities and other prominent sites. I admired the formality of everything, including bowing to one other, the exquisite food, especially fish and seafood, and the kindness of the people. I never tired of seeing the many temples, often with wonderful gardens, and loved the countryside more than Tokyo, where I spent a week, and which had become just another Westernized city that looks more American than Asian.

Traveling wasn't the only thing that occupied me during this time. I was also focused on finding a publisher for my book about reading Ulysses. I brought this up over breakfast with novelist Ann Patchett, and I also told her that making new friends was challenging at my age. She said she would call a literary agent, as well as her friend Jim Fox, and encourage both to reach out to me. The literary agent wasn't interested, but Jim was. He was the retired Chief Counsel at HarperCollins Publishers, a few years younger than me and as mischievous as Puck. It could also serve as the perfect nickname for Jim, who was as delightful and light-hearted as anyone could be. He was a dedicated movie buff who remembered every film he'd ever seen, including the names of the cast members, and he was an expert on the classic MGM musicals. He enjoyed singing and dancing in the old Hollywood style and said he sometimes regretted his decision to attend law school instead of pursuing a career in Hollywood.

We bonded easily during our regular lunch meetings. I shared my hopes of publishing my book on Ulysses—after all, he had worked in publishing all his life—and he was skeptical when I assured him that anyone determined could read it. Until then, he had avoided Joyce. He asked me to be his tutor, so we met weekly at his apartment to discuss the book, chapter by chapter. He was an excellent student. However, in what became his final weeks, he revealed that he had been diagnosed with pancreatic cancer, the disease that took my mother and Edgar. Despite his suffering, he was determined to finish reading the book. Although Jim completed seventeen of the eighteen chapters, he stopped just before the final chapter, Molly's soliloquy, a masterpiece of writing that would have truly delighted him. His sight had worsened, and despite his brave coping with the severity of his condition, he suddenly died a few days later. I miss his wit and wisdom, our debates over the meanings of Joyce's work, and performing his version of a scene from Scudda Hoo! Scudda Hay!, an absurd 1948 MGM musical. There will never be another Jim like him.

Chapter Eighteen:
My Life After Edgar

What was my life like after Edgar's death? My parents taught me that there is life and there is death and that both deserve my attention. They also encouraged me to understand that excessive grieving for the dead was futile. When my mother died, my father did not grieve her loss but longed for the companionship they had enjoyed for nearly fifty years. Perhaps it's a question of words; I don't know, but it is a very sensitive subject for survivors. I have written here only about my personal experience, respecting others and those who might disagree. I learned to accept death as inevitable, realizing that when a friend, parent, or partner dies, I can find peace without sorrow.

I stood beside Edgar's bed as he died, and before I left the hospital, a woman—a volunteer from the hospice service—approached me and asked if I would like to talk with her. She was not one of the so-called grief ladies who reportedly haunt the hospital halls. She assured me that she would listen, not offer advice. Her honesty and concern touched me, so we had a meaningful discussion. When friends later asked me what stage I had reached on the familiar list of grieving practices, I told them I did not follow that path. Instead, when I thought of Edgar, I remembered the forty wonderful years we had together.

Back in 1957, when I was a junior in college, I read the autobiography of Caitlin Thomas, the widow of poet Dylan Thomas.

Their life together had been abusive and unhappy, as suggested by the title of her book, Leftover Life to Kill. She wrote with pessimism and a sense of futility about her future. I saw mine as full of possibilities—new friends to make, trips to take, books to write—but I never felt like I was just biding my time until I died. I didn't cry, and while I was alone, I wasn't lonely.

Living in Manhattan

In a previous chapter, I reviewed the three apartments where I have lived in Manhattan on the Upper East Side. After Edgar asked me to move to an apartment closer to him, I leased one at The Bristol, where I am now happily settled. Although some pretentious tenants here enjoy bragging about living in the Sutton Place neighborhood, Sutton Place itself is a tiny enclave four blocks away. Of course, the name once indicated fame and fortune, so people tend to use it. Our building is located in Midtown Manhattan, an area extending from 34th Street to 59th Street and from Sutton Place to 8th Avenue.

Although I enjoy my solitude these days and take good care of myself, I miss Edgar but will not consciously seek out a new partner. I am in a state of what Samuel Beckett calls "lovelessness." Instead, I have cultivated friendships in the neighborhood, a microcosm of Midtown. John Ziebarth, who recently passed away at 87, was a friend of thirty years whom I met years ago in the Vanderbilt YMCA swimming pool. He lived in the nearby Beekman Place neighborhood and encouraged me to join a small group of mostly retired men who gather each Thursday morning for coffee at Tal's Bagels. I sit in the spot formerly occupied by Sal Piro, who also recently died. He led a flamboyant and successful life both in and out of show business. As his obituary in The New York Times stated, Sal was not only the "superfan" of The Rocky Horror Picture Show (1975) but also the founder of its international fan club and the author of two books about the film. After a few months, I recruited three new members to Bristol: Arnold Handler, a semi-retired tax attorney; Michael Doren, a retired but still very active artist; and Robert Attermann, another talent representative. The average age is in the early eighties. Our lively conversations cover the arts, politics, and humor. Of course, we refer to health problems but have discontinued what is known in such groups as an organ recital, shorthand for complaining about one's health.

Deborah Goldman, a neighbor at The Bristol and not a member of the coffee group, is a woman of many talents and accomplishments. Among these are her two successful children, a lifelong career as a psychologist, and now a dedicated effort to educate the public and raise funds for research on Adult Polyglucosan Body Disease (APBD). She and I meet often to discuss everything in our shared interests, from the best French restaurant in New York to travel, books, and movies. Although she is female and much younger, she has had a full life, and we have much in common.

As for the friends who have supported me in writing this book, Ron Hall has saved my life from the flames of computer hell. Writers are familiar with this fresh hell—a situation in which you know you have saved some written pages but cannot access them, or when the printer won't work or needs to be replaced, or when a computer program fails to meet your expectations, or when it's the end of a long day and technology, not you, has triumphed. I don't know what others do to handle these situations, but I call Ron Hall, President of Vibrant Muse and an Apple consultant for Cirque du Soleil, who comes to the rescue as quickly as Lassie did when saving that baby from a burning house—or was it a well? No kidding, Ron is an expert in solving problems far bigger than mine, yet he brings the same intelligence and experience to help me out of trouble. He works in both Montreal, the headquarters of Cirque, and New York City, where he has other clients. There is nothing related to computers that he cannot solve, and he always delivers exactly what I want or need. Ron is almost as tall and strong as Paul Bunyan but calm and witty in his work. Unlike so many computer experts, he is humble about his talents and manages all of this while also caring for his aging parents.

New Travel Adventures

I would now be traveling solo, and the first of these trips was suggested by Renato Tonelli, a colleague at Hunter College who was born in Italy and still owns the family house in Pontremoli, high in the Tuscan hills. He kindly invited me to spend time there in the summer with him, his wife, and his daughter. The rustic surroundings and relative isolation of the place allowed for relaxation, reading, and enjoying wonderful food. I spent ten days with them before taking a train to Bologna, my favorite Italian city, and then onward to Germany and the Netherlands.

As I mentioned earlier, Edgar wished for his ashes to be scattered in the Ganges River as it flows through the sacred city of Varanasi. I had no idea how to accomplish this in such a revered place, so a friend in Delhi connected me with Shailesh Tripathi, a college professor and Hindu priest residing in Varanasi. He assured me that non-Hindus are welcome to participate in the ashes ritual, and he made the necessary arrangements, including a young girl who placed orange marigolds and votive candles to float on the water. At sunrise, the priest conducted the rite while standing in an open rowboat, inviting me to join him in reciting prayers. Following that, after much twirling of incense, I scattered Edgar's ashes on the water. This lasted about thirty minutes as other boats drifted by and daily life continued along the shore. It was a deeply powerful moment when the priest proclaimed that Edgar had achieved moksha, the release of the soul from the body. Understanding my relationship with Edgar, the priest told me that I, too, was letting go—not of my soul, but of Edgar.

When I returned to the hotel, which had once been a Maharaja's palace, the staff, who remembered Edgar from previous visits, gathered to offer their condolences, followed by a lavish breakfast served in the garden as a gift from the hotel manager. Travelers returning from India often describe experiencing the country's unique aura of power, which encompasses the lingering traces of the British Raj's imperial influence and memories of books and movies that depict a fairytale India. I felt that power throughout the day. Following this unforgettable experience, I spent another four weeks traveling alone to unfamiliar parts of India, including villages and large cities that, unfortunately, have become so Westernized over the past thirty years that they have sacrificed their enchanting charm for other kinds of power: high technology and the wealth that comes with it.

Corsica

Then COVID hit, and to protect myself as much as possible, I spent almost three years in my apartment as much as possible. From this, I needed to escape to a place with constant sunshine where I could relax, read, and get a nice tan. Based on several prior visits, I believed Greece would be the right choice, but wanting something new, I chose instead the French island of Corsica (L'île de Corse). My 21-day itinerary began with a flight to Nice, followed by a forty-five-minute flight to Bastia-Poretta airport in Corsica. At the airport, I took a taxi driven by a man named Tintin, sent by my hotel in Oleta to greet me. Oleta is a hillside town with large houses—colored white, pink, or ochre—nestled into the forested hillsides. At A U Palazzu Serenu, a boutique hotel, I received a warm welcome and was assigned a spacious room with a sea view. After swimming a few laps, which were clumsy but sufficient, I had lunch on the terrace. Everything felt so quiet and peaceful, and then I realized I was the only guest.

Corsica, one of the 18 regions of France, is the fourth-largest island in the Mediterranean Sea, following Cyprus, Sicily, and Sardinia. Surrounded by the Ligurian, Mediterranean, and Tyrrhenian Seas, it is divided by a mountain range into northern and southern regions. Basking in glorious sunlight, my first impressions of the country were very positive. A car trip through the varied terrain is essential to truly appreciate the island's diverse beauty. Nature conservation is of great importance to the Corsicans, resulting in their creation of a bright, clean, and unpolluted paradise. The air is fragrant with the scents of magnolia, wild rosemary, and fennel, while walls everywhere are covered with cascades of vibrant bougainvillea. The high mountain ridges provide views of small coves and beaches, as well as passing ships, yachts, and pleasure boats.

After Oleta, I stayed at hotels in Florent, Monticello, Calvi, Corte, and Ajaccio, the capital of Corsica and the birthplace of Napoleon Bonaparte—a virtual shrine to him. For centuries, the island has been ruled by both Italy and France, a blend reflected in its culture. In some towns, the menu is Italian, along with the food and drinks; in others, it's French. Nevertheless, the Italian influence is evident in the presence of the Corse Mafia, which quietly engages in drug dealing and other criminal activities. Still, the island is considered safe for both travelers and residents. However, when I booked dinner at La Villa Calvi, the best hotel in town, my hotel concierge reminded me to carry my passport or another form of identification due to the hotel's heavy security. He didn't explain why. My car was stopped at the top of a long, steep driveway, and although the driver was recognized, I was asked to show my passport, which two very suspicious-looking guys examined. It felt like a scene from a James Bond movie, and when I had a drink at the bar before dinner, I noticed one of them watching me. When I went to the men's restroom two floors down, he followed me and kept watching until I returned to the dining room. I guess I passed his test because he eventually disappeared, giving me a strange sense of accomplishment. Throughout the island, the food was generally great. Fish and shellfish of all kinds, some unfamiliar, were available in abundance. A standout dish is the cured pork, raised on chestnuts and then roasted. The fruits and vegetables are freshly picked, and Brocciu, the island's softest goat cheese, holds its own among the traditional French and Italian cheeses. You will never go hungry in Corsica.

The Pacific Northwest

Later that same year, my sister Sue and I spent two weeks in early fall traveling by train through the Pacific Northwest, our first major trip together. She had lost her husband, Tom, shortly after I lost Edgar, and I hoped this journey would provide a pleasant change for her, so I asked her to choose the destination. Our main stops were Portland, Oregon; Seattle, Washington; and Vancouver, British Columbia, the westernmost province of Canada. The focus of the trip included gardens, museums, restaurants, their new cuisines, and the preservation of much of the indigenous Native American cultures. In that region, the weather is always unpredictable, shifting from sunshine to torrential rain and back again. The highlights of the trip were the Asian gardens, including Washington Park in Portland and the Washington Arboretum in Seattle, where the summer colors were just beginning to transition to autumn hues. The best museum is the University of British Columbia Museum of Anthropology in Vancouver, featuring a magnificent collection of native art that was carefully curated and displayed. As for food, the fish and shellfish were always market-fresh and beautifully presented. Some restaurants in Portland and Seattle have gained a reputation for their new American cuisine. However, there was little sign of genuine innovation in the restaurants we chose, with one exception: Altura in Portland, where the chef's menu offers a parade of small plates. The first dishes served are so unique and exquisitely presented that they would seem laughable if the staff didn't take them so seriously. For the main course, diners could choose either sautéed lingcod or seared duck breast. We each opted for the fish, which was a tiny piece of cod smaller than half a pack of cigarettes. And so on. The wine was excellent, the servers were efficient and charming, and the bill was outrageous for our indulgence in such exquisite silliness.

For me, a highlight of the Seattle trip was not visiting the Rock & Roll Hall of Fame, which is important, but reuniting with Liz Seder, a former colleague at The College of Staten Island. We had kept in touch for all those intervening years. At 93, she was as spry, sharp, and charming as ever, now living in a lovely assisted-living facility. We brought her books and, at her request, two bottles of wine and, afterward, enjoyed tea and cakes. She played a significant role in the early years of my career, and I was saddened to receive the news of her passing the year after this reunion.

We were looking forward to Vancouver, which has a reputation for having the best Chinese food outside of China. I don't know who claimed that. We chose the highest-rated restaurant but were disappointed by the bland dumplings they are known for. On the other hand, The Blue Water Café truly deserves its reputation for serving the best seafood in town, and our hotel, the Rosewood Georgia, has an excellent restaurant.

A highlight of this trip was taking a seaplane from Vancouver to Victoria Island, the capital of the province. We enjoyed strolling through the quiet streets on a perfect autumn day, yet there very few tourists. The return trip was on a beautiful, powerful ferry with only first-class seating. We were advised to keep an eye out for whales, but we didn't spot any. Sue and I parted ways at the airport the next day, with Sue heading to Los Angeles while my flight was rescheduled. So, we ended the trip with travel's typical ups and downs. Overall, this brother and sister got along well, enjoying ourselves through those highs and lows.

Belgium and Berlin

In 2019, I revisited Belgium, starting with three nights in Bruges, where walking is the best way to explore the city. At St. Salvatore Cathedral, I was terrified by Dieric Bouts's painting, "The Martyrdom of St. Hippolytus," which depicts the saint being pulled apart by four horses attached to his arms and legs. Following Bruges, I spent two nights in Ghent, where Van Eyck's "Mystic Lamb" altarpiece is a must-see, and then was off to Antwerp, where the food is exceptional, as it tends to be throughout Belgium. A highlight here is the Petershuis, the museum and gardens of Peter Paul Rubens, the Flemish master. For a remarkable contrast, visit architect Zaha Hadid's Port House building.

Next, on to Berlin, where on the first night I joined my friend Manu von Miller for a performance by the Vienna Philharmonic, conducted by Daniel Barenboim, playing music by Prokofiev and Mahler. I happily revisited the great museums, especially those on Museum Island. One evening, I joined my friends Buddy and Gesine for a concert by the Deutsche Symphonic Orchestra, with the renowned pianist Mitsuko Uchida performing Webern's variations. In Dresden, which I have always considered Germany's least friendly city, I began my visit with Bach's "St. Matthew Passion," performed by the Dresden Philharmonic Orchestra along with a choir of 200 voices (yes, I counted them). Art lovers always highlight the newly refurbished Green Vault in the Residenzschloss, showcasing a dazzling display of decorative arts.

Regarding food, one can eat very well in Dresden, particularly at Atelier Sanssouci. As the cab arrived in the wooded area where the restaurant was located, I noticed a prominent official-looking sign posted on a tree. One arrow pointed to Dachau, the other to Auschwitz—an unfriendly anti-Semitic warning. The dinner was exceptionally good.

The following day was Easter, and my return flight turned out to be one of those airport fiascos that one wants to forget, but I eventually landed at JFK that evening.

Finishing a Book

During all this foreign and domestic travel, I did not forget that I had to edit the final manuscript of my book about reading James

Joyce's Ulysses, a project with a long history. This final review resulted in many changes that I hoped would improve it. However, again, I found it impossible to engage a literary agent, which is necessary for initial contact with a publishing house. Efforts were made, but the advice I received was not encouraging. Nonetheless, I was determined to finish the manuscript and set it aside until the publishing climate might change in my favor. I know there have been other reader's guides to the novel, but mine is aimed at the general reader (i.e., the average person, not a college student or scholar). My approach is to act as a friendly companion and to anticipate all the questions such a reader might have. I believe that my approach encourages people to read it without fear. Finishing the book is a great accomplishment for any reader.

Revisiting Wales

I planned my next trip for two weeks in Wales, a country that requires a car and driver so that the tourist can see its extraordinary beauty without worrying about driving on what we consider the wrong side of the road. I placed a query on the web and was delighted to hear from Fiona Peel, who runs "Take Me to Wales," a travel agency. Although she has several drivers, she was the only one available for the period of my trip. Together, we agreed on an itinerary covering most of the country I had visited almost fifty years ago. Her knowledge of her country ensured that my trip would be perfect.

However, before visiting Wales, I stopped in London to see the exhibition titled "Van Gogh and Britain" at the Tate Britain gallery.

It explored the French artist's influence on both modern and contemporary British painters, and featured a surprising collection of three canvases by Francis Bacon, studies for a portrait of Van Gogh. After two days, on a clear and mild day, I took the train from London to Cardiff to meet Fiona for the first time. I found her to be petite, casual, and charming—a woman of great intellect with a wonderful sense of humor. We quickly became friends as we set off in her new Toyota hybrid sedan for a tour of Cardiff, including its public buildings, Cardiff Castle, the National Museum, and Castell Coch, a Gothic revival building with whimsical décor that is a delightful surprise. Later, I checked into St. David's Hotel on the waterfront, a very modern hotel primarily serving businesspeople. Although I hadn't requested it, I was given the top-floor master suite at standard room rates, offering enough space to host a large party and featuring floor-to-ceiling windows with a spectacular view of the harbor.

Wales is a multi-layered place, officially and politically connected to England and Scotland, yet it remains its own country, characterized by overwhelming natural beauty and serenity. Miles of narrow country roads wind through farms, with brilliant green fields enclosed by hedgerows. It's easy to love Wales, especially once you become accustomed to the ever-changing weather, particularly the almost daily rainfall, regardless of the season. However, summer is quite pleasant. The locals are friendly to tourists and eager to discuss your travels and impressions of the country. The coal mining industry and the culture it created have nearly vanished due to climate concerns, but deep mines still exist where shale is extracted for construction purposes. You can easily see the ruins of old coal mines and even visit some, or at least explore museums dedicated to the experience of what it was like to "go down the mine," as you may have heard in the movies. Those mines are central to the story of How Green Was My Valley (1941), John Ford's cinematic masterpiece that illustrates what those mines meant to the country's families, culture, and history.

Above ground, Wales is a country of castles—endless castles—and several magnificent cathedrals. I believe that St. David's Cathedral, located in the far west of the country, is the most inspiring and beautiful of them all. Every section and space has been created to be something different and impressive. Regarding the castles, there are more than six hundred of them in various stages of ruin, although you can visit some of their restored parts. When it comes to hotels, restaurants, and food, all are more than satisfactory. Hotels are typically small yet comfortable. The restaurants serve both hearty traditional dishes and modern cuisine. Whatever you choose, it's prepared with care and pride, not to mention delicious. The lamb, fish, and vegetable dishes are exceptional. Make sure to save room for the unique Welsh toffee desserts. You'll never go hungry in Wales.

The Welsh are known for their hearty drinking and vibrant pub culture. The pub is the heart of the village, and the abundant drinking may surprise tourists who are not accustomed to it. Nonetheless, the locals are incredibly welcoming to visitors. So, step into a pub and order a pint; you might even find yourself joining in the singing.

Fiona has become a good friend. She was born and raised in England and eventually married, moving to Wales, where she and her husband owned a working farm and raised three children. The name Peel holds significance in English history; her husband descends from Sir Robert Peel, who served as British Prime Minister twice during the 19th century. Fiona is deeply involved in civic matters, particularly health care for the underprivileged. For this and her other accomplishments, Queen Elizabeth II awarded her the OBE for outstanding public service. After royal titles, it is the highest honor one can receive in the UK.

A high point of this trip was meeting Jan Morris, the celebrated author of some fifty books on history, travel, personal life, and humor. While she is often considered a travel writer, her books are characterized by sharp observations and deep thinking that lean more toward a philosophy of life than simply informing readers where to find a good hotel or restaurant. When I met her, she was an active 93, living in the Welsh farmhouse she had shared with her wife for many years. It was a cold, rainy morning when I arrived to meet her for breakfast at the unique Portmeirion Hotel; she was dressed in a caftan with a heavy turquoise necklace around her neck. She drives herself in an aging Honda, and her reckless driving is so well-known in her area that she was required to notify the police whenever she went out for a drive so they could follow her to ensure she did not get into any trouble.

She is clearly serene and secure in her life decisions, content and happy with her achievements. Jan still reads widely and had three books published in the year I saw her! Since she loves Manhattan almost as much as she does Wales, I brought her gifts of a toy yellow cab, a recent New York Times article about her, and a jar of American marmalade, her breakfast favorite; indeed, she is an expert on the subject. She bid me farewell with a kiss on the cheek, saying, "Kindness is the only way to deal with the world." And then she was gone, kindness personified. As she drove out of the hotel grounds, I noticed a police car following her at a discreet distance. I feel very lucky to have spent two truly memorable hours with her on that dark and rainy Welsh morning. She died the following year.

Our Life Together

Although I made the trip to Wales in the fall of 2019, I was not overly concerned about the ongoing COVID situation. However, during the years 2020 to 2022, I felt it was too dangerous to travel. I followed all the recommendations, including vaccination and booster shots, and managed not to get infected. As a result, I was mostly homebound, going out with a mask and avoiding crowds. For several years, I had been an honorary member, along with Edgar, of the Visiting Committee of the Department of Drawings and Works on Paper at the Metropolitan Museum, and I enjoyed the meetings held four times a year in the department's fascinating laboratory. Not wanting to be late, I hurried across the museum's marble floors, but I slipped, fell, and injured my left shoulder. Nevertheless, I attended the meeting because I would never miss a presentation by Marjorie Shelley, the Director, who has a gift for making one appreciate the amazing work of her paper restoration staff, an achievement that is recognized worldwide.

Some weeks later, I underwent total shoulder replacement surgery at the Hospital for Special Surgery. Then, I began to recover with twice-weekly physical therapy sessions with Gregg Solomon. He did everything he could to enhance the rotary movement of my arm, but it still did not allow me to swim laps with any style. After two years of physical therapy of working with Gregg, he advised me to work with a personal trainer to strengthen my body. I found that person in José Solis, a trainer at the gym in The Bristol. Three mornings a week, I have spent an hour working out with him as he changes the routines, increasing the difficulty as I grow stronger. We worked together toward returning my left arm's full range of movement, but despite our efforts, my body would not let that happen. However, his belief in my ability and rigorous workout program has given me new confidence in myself both physically and psychologically.

Over the years, outside of the gym, José and I became friends. He has led an inspiring life, dedicated to his work, his clients, and the care and well-being of his two adolescent sons, who live with their mother. He has custody privileges and uses his time with the boys to introduce them to nature, museums, hiking, and a variety of food. He closely monitors their progress in school, applying the same intelligence and common sense to this responsibility as he does with his clients. While I have emphasized the importance of kindness in my writing, José exemplifies kindness in his everyday life. He is always there when you need him. He has inspired me to strive for a greater level of generosity and humanity in my life.

Lake Como, Italy

Weary of being housebound and wanting a break from the limitations placed on my life by COVID, surgery, and recuperation, I decided to visit Lake Como in Italy in September 2022. I gave myself a treat by booking a ten-day stay at the Grand Villa d'Este on the lakeshore, long known as one of the world's most luxurious hotels. The direct Emirates flight from JFK to Milan was smooth, and I spent two nights at the Hotel Principé de Savoia before taking a cab on the short drive to the little town of Cernobbio, about five miles from the hotel. Arriving, one is stunned by the hotel's size and grandeur, but that just gets better as days go by. The gardens and grounds could be a national park in themselves. The surrounding villages are surprisingly plain.

The origins of the Villa d'Este date back to the 15th century, and it has been remarkably well-preserved since becoming a hotel in the 1870s. Despite numerous modern improvements, it remains a reminder of a bygone era. When I checked in, I discovered that 100 guests were present for a grand wedding. The bride and groom hailed from Connecticut, and the bride's father, who served on the hotel's board of directors, arranged for a private jet to transport all these guests from New York and cover all their expenses. He also invited additional guests, like me, to observe the wedding ceremony and participate in activities such as the concerts. It was a genuine, thoughtful gesture that was warmly welcomed.

The wedding day was clear and warm, perfect for the outdoor ceremony held on the lawn under a canopy of roses from the hotel's nursery. This was followed by dinner outside beneath a canopy of twinkling lights. The men wore black ties, and the women appeared in floor-length dresses adorned with eye-catching jewelry. During dinner, guests enjoyed a concert featuring performances by soloists from La Scala in Milan. The evening before, there had been a concert with a prominent Italian rock band. The wedding dinner was followed by more dancing and then, at midnight, a spectacular hour-long fireworks display over the lake. The wedding guests took this lavish display in stride as they hailed from Greenwich, Southampton, and Locust Valley and expected nothing less.

My large room had every comfort imaginable, except for the separate shower I had requested when booking. After a friendly discussion with Francesca at the front desk, she moved me to a junior suite with a separate shower and a small terrace that enhanced my view of the lake. Considering that the wedding party left no spare rooms, this was serviced in grand style. I tried to make each day unique, but there was no shortage of things to do. You could walk for an hour around the well-kept grounds of the hotel, visit the expansive gardens and greenhouses, or rent a small private boat for a guided tour of the lakeshore. I took a boat to Bellagio, a charming village, and after exploring, enjoyed a very special lunch there. Alternatively, you could stay within the hotel gates, reading, soaking up the sun, enjoying a late afternoon English high tea, or simply admiring the elaborate flower arrangements in the main hall. You could also exercise in the gym or swim in one of the two pools, one indoors and the other lakeside. And you could, as I did every day, take a peaceful nap before dinner.

On my first evening, I wore a blue blazer since jackets were required for dinner. I enjoyed a perfect Negroni in the stylish Canova Bar and then entered the dining room, where I was surprised to see that many of the women were in formal attire, including one who wore an impressive tiara. She was likely the Queen of Connecticut. The men were more casual, some in jackets and others in shirt sleeves. The formally dressed waitstaff was so well-trained that they remembered your preferences, following the best European traditions, which made you feel very comfortable the next time you sat down in the elegant dining room. The menu and wine list were impressive; in addition to familiar Italian dishes, there was a complete continental menu. The food and wine were traditional and excellent. The breakfast buffet was far more extensive than the usual fare. A waiter asked me, "Caviar for your toast, sir?"

My last day at Villa d'Este arrived all too quickly. The weather was bright and beautiful each day, with no hint of rain. I hated leaving this special place and returning to reality. However, a cab took me to Milan Malpensa Airport for my Emirates flight back to New York.

Afterword

This account of my family, education, travels, achievements, work, play, sex, lovers, friends, encounters with celebrities, and thoughts on other subjects recollect a life well-lived and well-loved. It was fun to live it and write about it, and I hope you have enjoyed reading it.

The memories of the many years recalled in this chronicle reflect the experiences that have helped me to grow into the man that I am. But this is not the culmination of my story, for I continue to learn, grow, and change from new experiences. From the influence of my parents and teachers, I learned tolerance and kindness, qualities reinforced by friends as different as Bobby Short and Jan Morris. My father encouraged me to love diversity and freedom and to declare my homosexuality with pride. My other tried to shape my life to her viewpoint and was less successful.

From living in an inequitable world, I learned compassion and, as author Claire Keegan says, "…Is there any point in being alive without helping one another?" From Edgar, I learned love and respect in our partnership. My students taught me patience and tolerance, which helped me to write a college textbook that is now used by over 400 colleges. From the mentors of my career in university administration, I learned the importance of collegiality and compromise. And from my travels, I have learned more than I can say.

Orson Welles is known to have said that "a work is good to the degree that it expresses the man who created it." I hope I have met his standard. And, as the French say, Je ne regrette rien.

Manhattan, March 2025

www.ingramcontent.com/pod-product-compliance
Lightning Source LLC
LaVergne TN
LVHW010312070526
838199LV00065B/5529